Learning Games: Exploring the Senses Through Play

Other books by Jackie Silberg:

125 Brain Games for Babies: Simple Games to Promote Early Brain Development

125 Brain Games for Toddlers and Twos: Simple Games to Promote Early Brain Development

300 Three Minute Games: Quick and Easy Activities for 2-5 Year Olds

500 Five Minute Games: Quick and Easy Activities for 3-6 Year Olds

All About Me

Brain Games for Babies, Toddlers, and Twos: 140 Fun Ways to Boost Development

The Complete Book of Activities, Games, Stories, Props, Recipes, and Dances for Young Children: Over 600 Selections, with Pam Schiller

The Complete Book of Rhymes, Songs, Poems, Fingerplays, and Chants: Over 700 Selections, with Pam Schiller

Games to Play With Babies, Third Edition

Games to Play With Toddlers, Revised

Games to Play With Two-Year-Olds, Revised

Go Anywhere Games for Babies

Hello Rhythm: Rhythm Activities, Songs, and Games to Develop Skills

Hello Sound: Creative Music Activities for Parents and Teachers of Young Children

Higglety, Pigglety, Pop!: 233 Playful Rhymes and Chants

The I Can't Sing Book: For Grownups Who Can't Carry a Tune in a Paper Bag… But Want to Do Music With Young Children

I Live in Kansas

I Love Children Songbook

The Learning Power of Laughter

Let's Be Friends

Lollipops and Spaghetti Activity Book: Developmental Activities

My Toes Are Starting to Wiggle and Other Easy Songs for Circle Time

Peanut Butter, Tarzan, and Roosters Activity Book

Reading Games

Sing Yeladim

Sniggles, Squirrels, and Chickenpox: 40 Original Songs With Activities for Early Childhood

Songs to Sing With Babies

Learning Games Exploring the Senses Through Play

Jackie Silberg

Illustrated by Kathy Ferrell

Gryphon House, Inc.
Beltsville, Maryland

© 2006 Jackie Silberg
Published by Gryphon House, Inc.
10726 Tucker Street, Beltsville, MD 20705
800.638.0928; 301.595.9500; 301.595.0051 (fax)
Visit us on the web at www.ghbooks.com

The author of this book, Jackie Silberg, is an acclaimed speaker, teacher, and trainer on early childhood development and music. You can arrange to have her speak, present, train, or entertain by contacting her through Gryphon House, PO Box 207, Beltsville, MD 20704-0207, 800.638.0928, or at jsilberg@interserv.com.

 Gryphon House is a member of the Green Press Initiative, a nonprofit program dedicated to supporting publishers in their efforts to reduce their use of fiber sourced forests. For further information visit www.greenpressinitiative.org

Illustrations: Kathy Ferrell. Cover Art: Comstock Images.

Library of Congress Cataloging-in-Publication Data

Silberg, Jackie, DATE
Learning games : exploring the senses through play / by Jackie Silberg.
    p. cm.
  ISBN-13: 978-0-87659-007-2
  ISBN-10: 0-87659-007-5
  1. Perceptual learning. 2. Senses and sensation. 3. Early childhood education--Activity programs. I. Title.
  LB1067.S53 2006
  649'.55--dc22

                                   2005034840

Bulk purchase

Gryphon House books are available for special premiums and sales promotions as well as for fund-raising use. Special editions or book excerpts also can be created to specification. For details, contact the Director of Marketing at Gryphon House.

Disclaimer

Gryphon House, Inc. and the author cannot be held responsible for damage, mishap, or injury incurred during the use of or because of activities in this book. Appropriate and reasonable caution and adult supervision of children involved in activities and corresponding to the age and capability of each child involved is recommended at all times. Do not leave children unattended at any time.
  Observe safety and caution at all times.

Table of Contents

Introduction

The world is full of things to discover, things that delight the senses.

Explore these using your sense of hearing:
- sirens passing by
- rain falling softly
- thunder booming
- vibrations
- a whisper
- soft music

Discover these using your sense of sight:
- a beautiful rainbow
- family members
- books
- the letters of the alphabet
- birds in the trees
- flowers in a garden

Feel these using your sense of touch:
- hands
- textures
- warmth and coldness
- bubbles
- wet and dry

Sniff these using your sense of smell:
- flowers
- apple pies
- smoke
- smelly feet

Enjoy these using your sense of taste:
- ▶ yummy foods
- ▶ sweet, sour, salty, and bitter tastes
- ▶ yogurt
- ▶ chocolate

Follow your ears, eyes, nose, mouth, and hands as you explore the world every day through your senses.

CHAPTER 1

THE SENSE OF Hearing

Listen! What do you hear? The sound you hear may be as quiet as raindrops falling lightly. Or it may be loud, like a siren passing by. Sounds are everywhere, and you have two body parts that let you hear them all: your ears! Your ears collect sounds, process them, and send sound signals to your brain. And one more thing: your ears help you keep your balance!

The games in this chapter explore how ears work, how they identify sounds, and how the sense of hearing adds enjoyment and learning to life.

Interesting Facts About Ears, Sounds, and Hearing

▸ A humpback whale communicates with beeps and calls that sound like songs. A whale that is miles away can hear another whale's song.
▸ Companion dogs can be trained to identify many sounds, including the following: fire and smoke alarms, a telephone ring, a door knock, a doorbell, an oven timer, an alarm clock, a name being called, and a baby crying.
▸ Crickets hear with their legs; sound waves vibrate a thin membrane on the cricket's front legs.

▶ Some children and adults have difficulty hearing certain •
sounds. To help them hear better, they may wear
something in their ear called a *hearing aid*, which is a
small machine that they wear either inside or outside the
ear.

The following poem is about vibration, which is a
component of sound:

> *Vibration makes the air move,*
> *And that's what makes the sound.*
> *So listen, listen, listen*
> *There is sound all around.*
> —Jackie Silberg

Enjoy this funny poem about ears!

> *Where do you wear your ears*
> *Underneath your hat?*
> *Where do you wear your ears?*
> *Yes, ma'am, just like that!*
> *Where do you wear your ears?*
> *Tell me where, you sweet child,*
> *Where do you wear your ears?*
> *On both sides of my smile.*

Vibrations

Teaches how sounds feel in your throat

- Put your fingers on the front of your throat, very close to what is sometimes called your "voice box." Be careful not to press too hard.
- Make different sounds to feel the vibration of your larynx.
- Have your child talk, yell, hum, and whisper.
- Ask him to describe what he felt in his throat as the noise was coming out.

Read *Listen! Listen!: A Story About Sounds* by Barbara Shook Hazen.

Vibration Trick

Teaches how sound is produced

- Suggest that your child hold the palm of her hand in front of her face.
- Have her blow on her palm.
- As she is blowing, she moves the index finger of her other hand up and down through the air stream.
- Suggest that she listen to how the sound of the air changes as she moves her index finger up and down through it.

Read *Roar Like a Lion!: A First Book About Sounds* by Tiphanie Beeke.

Watch the Vibration

Teaches how sound is produced

- Sound is produced by the movement of the air, or vibration. An autoharp is a wonderful instrument for watching vibration and hearing sound at the same time.
- Pluck a long string and see it move back and forth as you listen to the sound. Pluck a short string—you can hear the high sound but can hardly see the string move because it is moving so fast.
- Do the same thing with a rubber band: stretch it using two hands.
- Ask your child to pluck the rubber band.
- Talk about how fast it is moving back and forth and how it sounds.
- Stretch it farther apart and pluck again. Point out that it is moving faster and the sound is higher! The tighter the stretch, the higher the sound.
- Now, move your hands closer together so that the rubber band is looser. Point out how it moves more slowly and the sound is lower.

Read *Listen! Listen!: A Story About Sounds* by Barbara Shook Hazen.

READ

Vibration Listening

Teaches listening skills

GROUP GAME
- Divide the children into two groups.
- Have one group lie on the floor with one ear on the ground.
- Have the other group jump up and down while the first group hears and feels the vibrations.

Read *Night Noises* by Mem Fox.

Which Sound Is Best?

Teaches listening skills

- Sound travels through solids better than through air.
- Ask your child to place one of her ears on a table and listen to the noise as you tap on the table.
- Now, ask her to move away from the table as you tap again.
- Which sound could she hear best?

Read *Toes, Ears, & Nose!* by Marion Dane Bauer.

Partner Listening

Teaches listening skills

▶ You will need an empty metal coffee can and an assortment of objects, such as clothespins, a penny, cotton balls, and so on.

▶ Ask your child to close his eyes.

▶ Put one of the objects in the metal coffee can, put the top on, and then shake the can.

▶ The child guesses the object in the can by the sound it makes.

▶ Try this with two objects in the can. Keep adding more objects.

▶ To make this game more challenging, place similar objects, such as a coin, a marble, and a magnet, in the metal can.

Read *The Listening Walk* by Paul Showers.

Sign Language

Teaches about sign language

- A person who cannot hear sounds is said to be deaf.
- People who are deaf use a different language for talking. They use their hands to talk to one another. This language is called Sign Language.
- Teach your child how to say "I love you" in sign language.

Read *Dina the Deaf Dinosaur* by Carole Addabbom.

Parts of the Ear

Teaches about the shape of the ear

- The ear has two parts: the outer ear and the inner ear.
- Using a mirror, ask your child to look at or feel his ear. Ask if he can see how his ear narrows into a tunnel-like shape.
- Ask your child:
  - Can you move your ears? (Your ears move when you raise your eyebrows.)
  - Can you turn your ears? (No, but animals can turn their ears. Both cats and dogs can turn their ears.)

Read *Ears* by Cynthia Fitterer Klingel.

Hands Over Ears

Teaches how ears hear sounds

- Talk about ears. Ask your child to touch each ear and count each ear as she touches it.
- Have your child put her hands over her ears and talk. Then ask her to take her hands away and talk. Ask her whether her voice sounds different.
- Have your child put her hands over her ears and sing a song. Then ask her to take her hands off of her ears and sing the same song. What was different?

Read *Horton Hears a Who!* by Dr. Seuss.

READ

A Song About Ears

Teaches humor

- Sing this funny song about ears.

Do your ears hang low?
Do they wobble to and fro?
Can you tie them in a knot?
Can you tie them in a bow?
Can you throw them over your shoulder
Like a continental soldier?
Do your ears hang low?

Do your ears flip-flop?
Can you use them for a mop?
Are they stringy at the bottom?
Are they curly at the top?
Can you use them for a swatter?
Can you use them for a blotter?
Do your ears flip-flop?

Are your ears real small,
Barely visible at all?
Do they look just like two peanuts
Stuck onto a bowling ball?
Can you store them in a thimble
When you're feeling rather nimble?
Are your ears real small?

Do your ears fall off
When you give a great big cough?
Do they lie there on the ground,
Or bounce up at every sound?
Can you stick them in your pocket
Just like Davy Crocket?
Do your ears fall off?

Read *Do Your Ears Hang Low?*
by Caroline Jayne Church.

READ

Different Words for Ear

Teaches about languages

- Learn the word for ear in different languages:
  - in Spanish it is *el oído*
  - in French it is *l'oreille*
  - in Italian it is *le orecchie*
- Make up a sentence about the ear and use a different language for ear. For example, say, "Here is my *oido*," and point to your ear, or say, "My *oreille* is very important," and point to your ear.

Read *Hearing* by Maria Rius.

Listen to the Water

Teaches about changing sounds

- You will need a metal spoon and three water glasses that are each at least six inches tall and all the same size.
- Place the glasses in a row. Pour water into each glass as follows: the first glass, one inch; the second glass, two inches, and three inches in the third glass.
- Gently tap each glass with the spoon. You will hear three different sounds!
- If you play the third glass first and go backwards, you will play the beginning of the song "Mary Had a Little Lamb."

- Experiment with the sounds by adding water to a glass or taking some water out of a glass. When you add more water, the sound will become higher. When you take out water, the sound will become lower.
- If you use colored water, you will have rainbow music.

Read *What Do Your Hear?* by Anne Miranda.

Bell Ringing

Teaches about loud and soft

- Fill five small envelopes with jingle bells. Put one bell in one envelope, two in the next, three in the third, four in the fourth, and five in the last.
- Seal all of the envelopes and ask your child to arrange the envelopes from the softest sound to the loudest sound.
- Sing "Jingle Bells" while shaking the envelopes.

Read *Jingle Bells* by Nick Butterworth.

Paper Plate Shakers

Teaches about rhythm

- For each shaker, you will need two sturdy paper plates.
- Place seeds or small pebbles on one of the plates and place the other plate on top of the first so that both eating surfaces of the plates are facing each other.
- Use masking tape to seal the plates together.
- Make more shakers with different materials or different amounts of the same material.

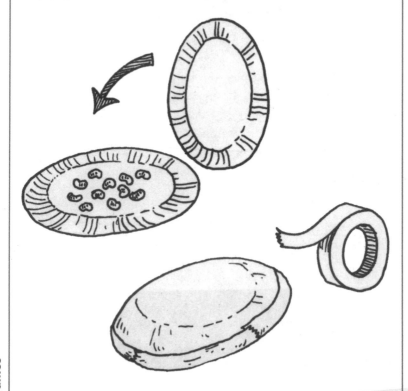

- Decorate the shakers with markers, glitter, construction paper, or ribbons.
- Shake the paper plate shakers. Ask your child, "Do the shakers make the same sound, or does each shaker make a different sound?"

- Play music and ask your child to select the paper plate shaker that makes a sound that goes with the music.

Read *The I Can't Sing Book: For Grownups Who Can't Carry a Tune in a Paper Bag But Want to Do Music With Young Children* by Jackie Silberg.

Can You Kazoo?

Teaches about vibration

- You will need a clean comb and a small piece of wax paper the same length as the comb.
- Holding the comb teeth-side down, fold the paper over the comb so that it covers both sides.
- Place one side of the comb to your mouth so that the paper is between your lips and the comb. Hum or sing against the paper.
- The vibration will cause a tingling sensation on your lips.
- Ask your child to describe the sound that this instrument produces.
- Once you get the hang of it, this is a lot of fun. The best part is that you can now play any song that you can hum. You don't even have to know the words!
- This is a version of a musical instrument called a kazoo.

Read *How to Kazoo* by Barbara Stewart.

Three Little Bears

Teaches how to compare sounds

- Read a book or tell the story of the "The Three Little Bears."
- Talk about the voices of the three main characters. Papa Bear has a *low* voice, Mama Bear has a *medium-pitched* voice, and Baby Bear has a *high-pitched* voice.
- Place three glasses exactly the same size on a table. Put water in each of the glasses: fill the first glass one-quarter full, the second glass half full, and the third glass completely full.
- Take a spoon and tap several times on each glass.
- Ask your child, "Which glass has a low voice like Papa Bear? Which one has a medium voice like Mama Bear? Which one has a high voice like Baby Bear?"

Read *Safari Sounds: Here and There* by Susan Ring.

Matching Sounds

Teaches auditory discrimination

- Divide eight empty film canisters into four pairs.
- Fill each pair with a different material, such as pennies, rice, paper clips, unpopped popcorn, sand, pebbles, or salt.
- Tape each canister shut.
- Ask your child to pick up one container and shake it.
- After she has listened to the sound, she can pick up each of the other containers and try to match the same sound.

▶ This game takes a lot of auditory discrimination and is excellent for developing listening skills.

Read Sounds on the Go! by Gail Donovan.

Newspaper Sounds

Teaches memory skills

- Demonstrate three things you can do to a newspaper: cut the paper, tear the paper, and crumple it.
- As you do each thing, ask your child to listen to the sounds.
- Turn your back to her, and do one of the three things. Ask her to listen and then tell you which of the three things you are doing.
- Switch roles and let your child tear, cut, or crumple the newspaper while you guess which action is making the sound.

Read *Paper Cutting Stories From A to Z* by Valerie Marsh.

Comparing Sounds

Teaches listening skills

- Fill a glass bottle with water and hit it gently with a metal object, such as a spoon. Listen to the sound.
- Pour out some water and hit the bottle again. Is the sound the same? (It will sound lower.)
- Keep pouring out water and hitting the bottle until it is empty. You will now have a low sound.
- Start pouring the water back and listen to the sound get higher.
- Depending on the age of your child, discuss the concept of vibration.

Read *You Can't Smell a Flower With Your Ear!* by Beverly Collins.

Ruler Sounds

Teaches about long and short and the relationship of each to sound

- Hold a ruler flat on a desk with half of it over the edge.
- Make a sound by pulling up the end of the ruler and letting it go. Do this by pressing down firmly on the part of the ruler over the desk with one hand, and then pulling up the part that hangs over the edge with the other hand.
- Ask your child the following questions:
  - Does the ruler move?
  - Does the ruler make a sound?
  - Can you hear the sound when the ruler stops moving?
- Adjust the length of the ruler over the edge of the desk. Pull it up and let it go again. Ask your child if the sound is the same as before.
- Listen with your child as the sound gets higher or lower.

Read *The Ear Book* by Al Perkins.

sproing!

Which Do You Hear?

Teaches auditory discrimination

▸ Take two film canisters or other small containers and fill one with salt and one with unpopped popcorn kernels.
▸ Shake each canister and listen to the sounds.
▸ Ask your child to cover her eyes while listening to the sounds and to identify which contains salt and which contains popcorn kernels.
▸ Ask her to cover one ear as she listens. Ask if there is a difference in the sound when she uses both ears.

Read *The Very Quiet Cricket* by Eric Carle.

What Are You Tapping?

Teaches listening skills

▸ Select five objects to tap with a wooden spoon.
▸ Ask your child to listen each time the spoon is tapped and to tell you what is being tapped.
▸ Now ask him to close his eyes as you tap one of the five objects again and see if he can identify the sound.

Read *The Best Ears in the World* by Claire Llewellyn.

The Sounds of Food

Teaches concentration skills

- Foods make different sounds.
- Listen to the sounds different foods make when they are chewed, such as potato chips, celery sticks, carrots, and a piece of toast.
- Now ask your child to close her eyes and see if she can identify each food by the sound it makes when you eat it.

Read *Bunny's Noisy Book* by Margaret Wise Brown.

READ

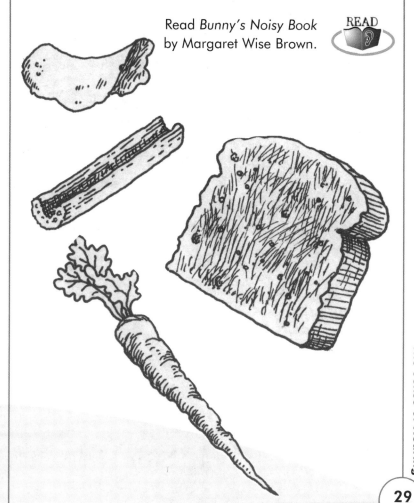

Hearing Day

Teaches cognitive skills

- Collect everyday items that make a noise.
- Listen to the noise each item makes.
- Put all of the items on a table.
- Ask your child to close her eyes.
- Make a noise with one of the items.
- See if she can identify the sound.

Read *Eyes and Ears* by Seymour Simon.

Rhythm Instruments

Teaches about loud and soft

- Gather all of the rhythm instruments you can find, such as rhythm sticks, a triangle, bells, cymbals, drums, castanets, guiro, and others.
- Play each instrument and talk about the sound each makes. Ask your child if it is loud or soft.
- Ask your child to arrange the instruments in order from the one that make the softest noise to the one that makes the loudest noise.

Read *Sound: Loud, Soft, High, and Low* by Natalie M. Rosinsky.

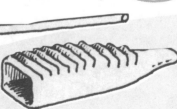

Listening to Paper

Teaches listening skills

- Start with several kinds of paper, such as newspaper, tissue paper, tissues, and cardboard.
- Tear each one as your child listens to each sound.
- Talk about the difference in the sounds.
- Have your child use the scraps to make a collage.

Read *Listen to the Rain*
by Bill Martin, Jr. and John Archambault.

Seashells

Teaches language skills

- Seashells are wonderful; each one is unique.
- Have your child say the following and listen for the /s/ sound.

  She sells seashells by the seashore.
  Where are the seashells she sells?

- Have your child hold a shell to his ear and listen for the ocean sound, although it is really the sound of his heartbeat.

Read *Seashells by the Seashore*
by Marianne Berkes.

Outside Sounds

Teaches listening skills

- While outside, sit on a bench or on the ground and listen for sounds.
- As your child names each sound, write it down.
- You will be surprised at all the noises you can hear when you are paying attention. Ask your child what she hears. Wind? Cars? Airplanes? Try to identify at least five different sounds.
- Once you have identified five different sounds, ask your child to try to duplicate the sounds with her voice when you are indoors.
- Repeat this at a different time and place, and listen for five new sounds.

Read *Too Much Noise* by Ann McGovern.

Seasonal Sounds

Teaches vocabulary

- Each season provides lovely hearing experiences.
- In the winter, you can listen to:
  - the quiet of falling snow
  - the sounds of ice cracking on a tree branch
  - the sound of your feet walking in the snow
- In the spring, you can listen to:
  - birds chirping
  - rivers and streams bubbling along
- In the summer, you listen to:
  - crickets and other noisy insects
  - water splashing at a swimming pool or fountain

▶ In the fall, you can listen to:
  ▶ the crunch of leaves
  ▶ leaves as they fall off the trees

Read *Sounds of a Summer Night*
by May Garelick.

Places and Sounds

Teaches memory skills

▶ Talk about the sounds of different places.
▶ Ask:
  ▶ What sounds do you hear at a baseball game?
  ▶ What sounds do you hear in the morning?
  ▶ What sounds do you hear at a restaurant?
  ▶ What sounds do you hear at school?

Read *Mr. Brown Can Moo, Can You?*
by Dr. Seuss.

Guess Who!

Teaches listening skills

GROUP GAME

▶ Sit in a circle.

▶ One child volunteers to wear a blindfold and sit in the middle of the circle.

▶ Silently select another child to make a soft noise, such as tapping his fingers on the floor.

▶ The blindfolded child points in the direction of the noise.

▶ Each child takes a turn guessing the direction of the noise while sitting in the center of the circle blindfolded.

Read *Sounds of a Summer Night* by May Garelick.

A Tape Recorder Game

Teaches memory skills

▶ Record sounds that take place in a particular place. For example, in the kitchen, tape record water running, dishes clattering, and a mixer or blender running.

▶ Play the tape and see how many sounds your child can identify.

▶ Do the same for outside sounds. You can record the sounds of cars, birds, and a garage door opening.

▶ Ask your child to identify the sound and tell you where the sound can be found.

Read *There Is a Carrot in My Ear and Other Noodle Tales* by Alvin Schwartz.

Shake, Tap, Clap!

Teaches sound recognition

- Ask your child to close his eyes and identify the sounds he hears.
- Make some of the following sounds:
  - shake coins
  - clap hands
  - tap a pencil or pen on a table
  - close a book
  - crumple up paper or foil
  - stomp on the floor
  - jump up and down
- Give him a turn to make the sounds while you close your eyes and then guess the sound.

Read *Why Mosquitoes Buzz in People's Ears: A West African Tale* by Verna Aardema.

Name the Sound

Teaches language skills

GROUP GAME

- Ask the children to take turns making a sound for the other children to identify.
- As each child chooses a sound, record it on a list.
- This list will enable you to play this game again by pointing to a sound and asking the children to make that sound.

Read *Dog's Noisy Day* by Emma Dodd.

Where Is the Sound?

Teaches spatial thinking

- Have your child close her eyes and listen carefully.
- Ask your child what sound she hears, and where that sound is coming from.
- Ask your child if the sound is high or low and if it is coming from the front of the room, the back of the room, from inside, or from outside.
- Ask your child if the sound is staying in the same place or traveling somewhere else.
- Sounds can be coughing, footsteps, a clock ticking, a door slamming, or even someone breathing.
- Talk about each of the sounds.

Read *I Thought I Heard* by Alan Baker.

What's Your Favorite?

Teaches respect for the ideas of others

GROUP GAME

- Talk about favorite sounds, such as laughter, music, a friend's voice, and so on.
- Ask each child to describe his or her favorite sound and why that sound is a favorite.

Read *Annabelle's Wish: My Favorite 10-Sound Story* by Michael Stewart.

Identifying Sounds

Teaches about vocabulary

GROUP GAME

▶ Talk with children about what makes sounds different and distinct.

▶ For example, what makes a sound scary, loud, soft, happy, or sad?

▶ Can a sound have two different meanings? For example, can crying mean both happiness and sadness?

Read *Flop Ear* by Guido Van Genechten.

A Sound Picture

Teaches thinking skills

▶ Look through magazines with your child and find things that make sounds, such as animals, cars, kitchen appliances, and so on.

▶ Ask your child to cut out pictures of things that make sounds and paste them onto a large piece of construction paper.

▶ If the child is too young to cut, let her choose the picture and you do the cutting.

▶ When you are finished, point to each picture and try to make its sound.

Read *Sounds on the Go!* by Gail Donovan.

Loud and Soft

Teaches motor skills

- This game is fun to play!
- Ask your child to perform different actions both loudly and softly. Suggestions include walking, singing, hopping, running, chewing, marching, and laughing.
- This game asks your child to think about hearing in a different way.

Read *The Indoor Noisy Book* by Margaret Wise Brown.

Listen to the Voice

Teaches about the direction of sound

GROUP GAME
- Sit in a circle.
- Blindfold one child and have him sit in the middle of the circle.
- Explain that when you point to a child, he or she is to say the name of the person who is seated in the middle of the circle.
- Point to a child and ask that child to say the name of the person in the middle.
- Ask the child in the middle of the circle to point in the direction of the voice and identify the name of the person who said his name.

Read *Sound: Loud, Soft, High, and Low* by Natalie M. Rosinsky.

Imitating Sounds

Teaches listening skills

- Make a sound and ask your child to imitate the sound.
- Ideas include coughing, laughing, crying, pretending to sneeze, singing "la, la" in a high voice, singing "la, la" in a low voice, singing "la, la" in a soft voice, singing "la, la" in a loud voice, and making a "raspberry." (I know you can think of many more sounds!)
- This game develops auditory discrimination skills.

Read *Daisy Says "Here We Go 'Round the Mulberry Bush"* by Jane Simmons.

Clap, Pat, Stomp

Teaches listening skills

- Ask your child to clap her hands and listen closely to the sound.
- Now, ask her to gently pat her hands together and listen to that sound.
- Finally, ask her to stomp her feet and listen to that sound.
- Then ask her to close her eyes.
- Choose one of the sounds she made, make that sound, and ask her to guess which sound you are making.
- Now, let her make the sound and see if you can guess the sound.

Read *Gerald McBoing Boing Sound Book* by Dr. Seuss.

Repeat What You Hear

Teaches sequencing skills

▶ Tell your child that you are going to say two words.
▶ Ask him to listen to the words and then repeat them.
▶ It is a good idea to start this game with rhyming words because they will be easier for your child to hear and remember. For example, start by saying "cat" and "mat."
▶ Ask him to repeat those words.
▶ Now add a third word—"cat," "mat," and "fat."
▶ Continue, saying as many words as he can hear and remember.

Read *The Best Ears in the World* by Claire Llewellyn.

Listen Carefully

Teaches about tone

▶ Explain to your child that you will ask a question and that you want her to answer "yes" or "no" in the same voice you use.
▶ For example, ask, "Do you like lollipops?" She answers, "Yes, I like lollipops." If you ask the question in a soft voice, the child will answer in a soft voice.
▶ Encourage her to imitate the sound of your voice as she answers you.
▶ Different ways to speak include loudly, softly, quickly, sweetly, gruffly, slowly, in a whisper, and in a nasal voice.

Read *Hear Your Heart* by Paul Showers.

Gossip

Teaches auditory discrimination

GROUP GAME

- ▶ This popular game, also known as "Telephone," helps children understand the importance of listening.
- ▶ Sit in a circle.
- ▶ Choose three words to whisper into a child's ear. Start with something easy like "Happy New Year."
- ▶ That child repeats what he heard in the next person's ear.
- ▶ When the words reach the last person, she repeats aloud what she heard to the group.

Read *The Very Quiet Cricket* by Eric Carle.

READ

Hearing Words

Teaches listening skills

- Select a poem or song that repeats the same word many times. For example, "Humpty Dumpty" or "Mary Had a Little Lamb."
- Tell your child that when she hears that special word (for example, "lamb"), she should jump up and down.
- An older child can listen for words that start with a certain sound, for example /l/.
- This is a wonderful listening experience.

Read *What Do Your Hear?* by Anne Miranda.

Hearing Instrument

Teaches cognitive skills

- Make a recording of your child singing a familiar song.
- Record him singing the same song a second time; this time, add musical accompaniment, such as a drum, a piano, rhythm sticks, or any other instrument.

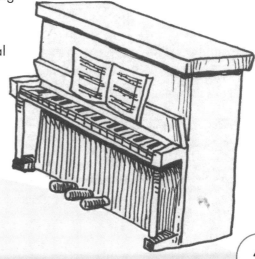

- Play the tape back and ask him which version had the musical accompaniment.
- If you have access to more than one musical instrument, continue making recordings with additional instruments and then try to identify the instruments by sound.

Read *Listen! Listen!: A Story About Sounds* by Barbara Shook Hazen.

Listening to Voices

Teaches how to identify and compare voices

- Play vocal music for your child. Select a variety of music with many different kinds of voices.
- Some ideas for listening include a male voice, a female voice, a child's voice, a high voice, a low voice, a children's chorus, and an adult chorus.
- Talk about how voices sound different. Ask your child to describe the different voices she hears.

Read *Polar Bear, Polar Bear, What Do You Hear?* by Bill Martin, Jr.

Listen Closely

Teaches cognitive skills

GROUP GAME
- Tell the children you are going to say two words.
- Tell the children if the words sound the same, they should hold up their thumbs.
- If the words sound different, they should keep their hands in their laps.
- Begin with words that sound clearly different (for example, dog and book) and move on to words that sound clearly the same (for example, where and wear).
- As the children develop their listening skills, make this game more challenging.
- This game requires very careful listening skills.

Read *Horton Hears a Who!* by Dr. Seuss.

Voice Sounds

Teaches creativity

GROUP GAME
- Ask the children to name the different sounds they can make with their voices, such as singing, screaming, coughing, crying, laughing, whispering, yelling, gargling, and so on.
- Write each sound on chart paper.
- After the list is made, count the number of sounds and then try to make each of the sounds on the list.

Read *The Monster Book of ABC Sounds* by Allan Snow.

Name That Voice

GROUP GAME

- Have one child sit with his back to the rest of the children.
- Select three other children who will all say the name of only one of the three children.
- For example, if the name of one of the three children is "Alexandra Menotti," each of the three children, including the real Alexandra, will take a turn and say, "My name is Alexandra Menotti."
- Ask the child who is sitting with his back to the others to identify which voice belongs to the real Alexandra Menotti.

Read *Do Your Ears Hang Low?* by Caroline Jayne Church.

Who Said That?

Teaches listening skills

GROUP GAME

- Sit in a circle.
- Ask everyone to close their eyes. Select one child to say "good morning" in a disguised voice.
- Ask the other children to identify the voice.
- Continue, giving each child a turn.

Read *My First Book of Sounds* by Golden Books.

Hello, How Are You?

Teaches fun

GROUP GAME

- This fun game uses a tape recorder.
- Record each child in the group saying, "Hello, how are you?" into a tape recorder.
- When everyone has had a turn, play the tape back to the group.
- Listen to each voice and ask the children to try to identify who is talking.

Read *Seashells by the Seashore* by Marianne Berkes.

Loudest Sound

Teaches about comparisons

- Suggest that your child make the highest sound she can with her voice.
- Do the same with the lowest sound, the softest sound, and the loudest sound.

Read *Sound: Loud, Soft, High, and Low* by Natalie M. Rosinsky.

Hearing Loud and Soft

Teaches listening skills

- Play instrumental music.
- Ask your child to listen for soft sounds and loud sounds.
- If the sound is soft, ask him to squat down on the ground.
- If the sound is loud, ask him to stand up straight and put his arms high into the air.

Read *Clifford's Animal Sounds* by Norman Bridwell.

What Do You Hear?

Teaches auditory discrimination

GROUP GAME

▶ Play a short piece of instrumental music for a group of children.

▶ When it is over, ask the children what kinds of sounds they heard. Ask the children if the sounds were fast, slow, loud, soft, high, or low.

▶ Ask one of the children to choose her favorite sound the next time the music is played. When she hears that sound, ask her to do a favorite action like jumping, clapping, or any other movement that she thinks suits the sound of the music.

▶ Continue to ask each child to choose a sound and do an action. The more the children listen for different sounds, the better their auditory skills.

Read *Sound: Loud, Soft, High, and Low*
by Natalie M. Rosinsky.

Do You Hear the Music?

Teaches movement

GROUP GAME

▶ Play a recording on a cassette or CD player. Instrumental music is best.

▶ Stop and start the music. Explain that the children should walk when they hear the music and freeze like a statue when they hear the music stop.

- Start the music again, and while it is playing, ask the children to tiptoe around the room while the music is playing. When the music stops, they again freeze in place.
- Play the music again; this time play it loud and then soft. Ask the children to stamp their feet when the music is loud and tiptoe when the music is soft.
- Young children really enjoy the "freeze" concept. This is a good word to use when you are trying to quiet down a noisy group.
- Another fun thing to do is to ask the children to identify what each child's frozen statue looks like.

Read *The I Can't Sing Book: For Grownups Who Can't Carry a Tune in a Paper Bag But Want to Do Music With Young Children* by Jackie Silberg.

Musical Chairs

Teaches movement

GROUP GAME

▶ Arrange the chairs in the middle of the room with the backs of the chairs touching. ▪

▶ Explain that to play this game the children walk around the group of chairs while the music is playing and then sit down on a chair when the music stops.

▶ Tell them there will always be one chair less than the number of children playing the game.

▶ Whoever does not find a chair sits on the floor.

▶ When everyone is sitting on the floor, the game is over.

Read *The Listening Walk* by Paul Showers.

Mother, May I?

Teaches coordination and listening skills

GROUP GAME

▶ One child is "Mother" and stands in front of the other children.

▶ The other children line up in a straight line facing Mother.

▶ Mother chooses a child and gives a direction for moving. For example, "Alisha, you may take one giant step forward."

▶ Alisha responds, "Mother, may I?" Mother then says, "Yes."

▶ If the child forgets to ask, "Mother, may I?" she must go back to the starting line.

▶ The first child to touch Mother becomes the next "Mother."

- There are many varieties of steps you can take:
  - baby steps
  - regular steps
  - scissors step—jump while crossing your feet, then jump while uncrossing them
  - bunny step—a hop

Read *Mother, May I?* by Lynn Plourde.

Dog and Bone

Teaches concentration skills

GROUP GAME

- Choose one child to be the dog and have her sit in a chair with her back to the rest of the children.
- Put an eraser or another object—the bone—under the dog's chair.
- While the dog is sitting with her eyes closed, someone sneaks up and takes the bone and hides it somewhere on himself. The dog keeps her eyes closed and tries to listen for a sound that will identify the person who is taking the bone.
- The dog opens her eyes, and the children chant:

  Doggy, doggy, where's your bone?
  Someone took it from your home.

- The dog has three chances to guess who took the bone.
- If the dog guesses correctly, she gets to be the dog again. If she guesses incorrectly, the child who had the bone gets his turn as the dog.

Read *The Very Quiet Cricket* by Eric Carle.

The Lion Game

Teaches concentration skills

GROUP GAME

- This game is best for children five years and older.
- Choose a child to be "Lion."
- Lion sits on a chair with his back to the other children, who are at least ten feet away.
- Put a stuffed animal behind Lion and tell Lion to pretend it is his cub.
- The other children take turns sneaking up behind the Lion and trying to take the cub.
- If Lion hears the person sneaking up, he can roar and then turn around, catching the child who is sneaking up. If Lion catches a child, that child takes Lion's place and Lion goes back with the other children.
- If there is no child when Lion roars, Lion remains in the chair and the game starts again.

Read *Roar Like a Lion!: A First Book About Sounds* by Tiphanie Beeke.

READ

Soft and Loud Songs

Teaches about loud and soft

- Sing favorite songs in a soft voice and in a loud voice.
- Some suggestions are "Twinkle, Twinkle Little Star," "Mary Had a Little Lamb," "Do You Know the Muffin Man?" and "Jingle Bells."
- Talk about the differences in sound, and even meaning, between the soft version and the loud version.

Read *Pick Me Up! Fun Songs for Learning Signs* by Sign2Me.

Drawing to Music

Teaches creative thinking

- Give your child crayons and paper and encourage him to draw to the music.
- Play instrumental music that has both fast and slow parts.
- Play instrumental music that is both loud and soft.
  Note: It is important that the music be instrumental music only, with no words, because the words detract from children's thought processes.
- Ask your child which kind of music he liked best.

Read *A Day in the Life of a Musician* by Linda Hayward.

Fan Sounds

Teaches about vibration

▶ Show your child how to fold a piece of paper like a fan.
▶ Ask your child to wave the fan in front of her face and say "hello."
▶ Ask your child to describe how the movement of the air changes the sound of the word.

Read *The Ear Book* by Al Perkins.

Guessing Body Sounds

Teaches about body sounds

GROUP GAME

▶ Talk with the children about the different sounds a body can make, including:
  ▸ feet sounds—stomping, hopping, jumping, sliding
  ▸ hand sounds—clapping, snapping, tapping, patting
  ▸ mouth sounds—whisper, yelling, whistle, clicking
▶ Ask the children to close their eyes.
▶ Make one of the sounds you have talked about.
▶ Whoever guesses the answer makes the next sound.

Read *Singing a Song: How You Sing, Speak, and Make Sounds* by Steve Parker.

I've Got a Rhythm

Teaches about rhythm

▶ Say the following chant. At the end of it, clap a rhythm with your hands or stamp a rhythm with your feet.

▶ Ask your child to listen and copy what you do. For example, if you clap three times, she should clap three times.

I've Got a Rhythm by Jackie Silberg
I've got a rhythm.
Listen to my rhythm.
I've got a rhythm.
Can you do it too?

Read *The Complete Book of Rhymes, Songs, Poems, Fingerplays, and Chants* by Jackie Silberg and Pam Schiller.

READ

Little Sir Echo

Teaches about echoes

- Talk about echoes and practice making them with your child.
- Recite the following poem. Say the echoes (in parentheses) in a soft voice.

  Little Sir Echo, how do you do?
  Hello (hello), Hello (hello)
  Little Sir Echo, I'm calling you.
  Hello (hello), Hello (hello)
  Hello (hello), Hello (hello)
  Won't you come over and play (and play)?
  You're a sweet little fellow.
  I know by your voice,
  But you're always so far away.

Read *Bunny's Noisy Book* by Margaret Wise Brown.

READ

The Copycat Game

Teaches listening skills

GROUP GAME

- Make a sound with your voice.
- Ask the children to listen and then make the same sound.
- Repeat the first sound and add another. For example, a cough and then a singing tone.
- Ask the children to listen and then make the same sounds.

- Continue, adding a new sound each time.
- Make this game more challenging by using sound and movement together.

Read *Nina, Nina and the Copycat Ballerina* by Jane O'Connor.

Strawberry Shortcake

Teaches listening skills

GROUP GAME

- Children need to use their ears and their listening skills for this game.
- Have all of the children stand in a circle. When each child hears his or her name, he or she should jump into the circle.
- When children hear their age, they should jump out of the circle.

Strawberry shortcake
Huckleberry Finn,
When you hear your name
You jump in. (say the name of a child)

Strawberry shortcake
Huckleberry Finn,
When you hear your age
You jump out. (say a number)

Read *Listening Games for Pre-Readers* by Lloyd Harnishfeger.

Learning Games

The Timer Game

- Set a timer, starting with 60 seconds, and hide it somewhere in a room.
- Have your child try to find the timer before it rings.
- You can shorten the time as he gets better at the game.

Read *The Indoor Noisy Book* by Margaret Wise Brown.

The Wake-Up Bell

- You will need a bell to play this game.
- Tell your child to pretend to be sleeping and then to wake up when she hears a bell ring.
- First let your child be the sleeper and you ring the bell; then reverse roles.
- To make it more fun, pretend to be an animal. When you wake up, make that animal's sound.

Read *Sounds on the Farm* by Gail Donovan.

Listening for Start and Stop

Teaches coordination

- Pick two noisemakers, such as a bell and a drum.
- Ask your child to walk when he hears the bell and to stop when he hears the drum.
- This game demonstrates the importance of silence as well as of sound.

Read *Sounds on the Go!* by Gail Donovan.

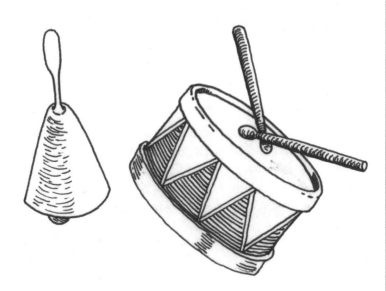

Whistle Game

Teaches fun

GROUP GAME

▶ Ask all of the children to close their eyes.

▶ Quietly give one child a whistle and ask him to hide.

▶ Tell him that when he finds a hiding place he should blow the whistle.

▶ Ask the other children to follow the sound of the whistle to find the hidden child.

▶ The child who finds the hidden child is next to hide.

▶ Children enjoy this game very much.

▶ This game is fun to play inside and outside.

Read *Annabelle's Wish: My Favorite 10-Sound Story* by Michael Stewart.

Make the Sound

Teaches about animal sounds

▶ This is a fun game for children who are just beginning to learn about animals.

▶ Pass out animal stickers or small stuffed animals, and encourage your child to imitate the sound the animal makes.

▶ She can also move like that animal.

Read *Clifford's Animal Sounds* by Norman Bridwell.

Old MacDonald

Teaches sequencing skills

▶ Sing the song "Old MacDonald Had a Farm."

▶ Pick three animals to use in the song. A cow, a horse, and a pig are animals children especially enjoy.

▶ Sing the song yourself and when you name one of the animals, ask the children to make that animal's sound.

▶ Continue to add more animals to the song. Let the children tell you which animals they want to imitate.

Read *Too Much Noise* by Ann McGovern.

Cats, Dogs, and Ducks

Teaches about animal sounds

GROUP GAME

▶ Choose three sounds. Animal sounds, such as the sounds a cat, a dog, and a duck, are good to start with.
▶ Let the children practice the individual sounds.
▶ Now, choose one child to make one of the sounds and let the rest of the group identify which sound they hear.

Read *Sounds of a Summer Night* by May Garelick.

Careful Listening

Teaches about animal sounds

GROUP GAME

▶ Select three children to come to the front of the room. Ask each child to choose an animal sound to make.
▶ With their backs turned to the class, ask all three children to make their sounds over and over at the same time until you say, "Stop."
▶ Now, ask the children which sounds they heard. As each correct sound is identified, have the sound maker sit down.
▶ When all of the sounds have been identified, select three more children to play the game.
▶ This is a marvelous listening experience.

Read *There Is a Carrot in My Ear and Other Noodle Tales* by Alvin Schwartz.

"Moo," Says the Cow

Teaches listening skills

GROUP GAME

▸ Ask one child to cover his eyes with his hands while sitting in a chair in front of the group.

▸ Select another child. Ask the entire group to say the first three lines of the following rhyme, and then choose one child to say the last line.

> *"Moo," says the cow.*
> *"Baa," says the lamb.*
> *Tell me, tell me,*
> (one child says) *Who I am?*

▸ The child who is covering his eyes guesses which child said the last line.

Read *Mr. Brown Can Moo, Can You?*
by Dr. Seuss.

Animal Voices

Teaches about loud and soft

- Talk with your child about animal sounds. Ask her which animals make loud sounds and which animals make soft sounds.
- Animals that make loud sounds include lions, seals, cows, tigers, and bears. Animals that make soft sounds include ducks, birds, chickens, rabbits, frogs, and owls.
- Ask your child to make a loud animal sound and then a soft animal sound.
- Ask your child to try making the sounds of the different animals.
- Ask, "Do some animals make both loud and soft sounds?" "Do you?"
- Look at pictures of zoo animals and talk about zoo animals that make loud and soft sounds.
- If possible, visit a local zoo.

Read *Merry-Go-Sounds at the Zoo* by Patricia Benton.

 READS

Frog Sounds

Teaches about languages

- Ask your child to pretend to be a frog, making the sound "ribbit, ribbit."
- Explain that children in other countries make different sounds when they pretend to be a frog.
- Have your child try the frog sounds listed on the next page.

Afrikaan: kwaak-kwaak
Arabic (Algeria): gar gar
Catalan: cruá-cruá
Chinese (Mandarin): guo guo
Dutch: kwak kwak
English (GB): croak
Finnish: kvak kvak
French: coa-coa
German: quaak, quaak
Hebrew: kwa kwa
Hungarian: bre-ke-ke
Italian: cra cra
Japanese: kerokero
Korean: gae-gool-gae-gool
Russian: kva-kva
Spanish (Spain): cruá-cruá
Spanish (Argentina): berp
Spanish (Peru): croac, croac
Swedish: kvack
Thai: ob ob (with high tone)
Turkish: vrak vrak
Ukrainian: kwa-kwa

READ

Read *Freddie Frog* by Emma George.

Animal Ears

Teaches about animals

- Ask your child which animal she thinks has the best hearing. Cat? Squirrel? Dolphin? The answer is the dolphin.
- Show your child pictures of a dolphin. Although their ear holes are tiny—about the size of a crayon point—dolphins have the best hearing because they receive sounds through their jawbone and head, and the vibrations pass into the tiny bones of their inner ear.
- Ask your child to touch her jawbone and move her fingers up to her ears.
- Ask her to do the same as she talks.

Read *Dolphins at Daybreak* by Mary Pope Osborne.

Dolphin Talk

Teaches about communication

- Dolphins use clicking sounds and whistles to communicate with one another.
- In addition to clicks and whistles, researchers have described dolphin sounds as screams, calls, moans, trills, grunts, squeaks, and even a "creaky door" sound.
- Researchers who study bottlenose dolphins think that slow clicks and high-pitched whistles are signs of contentment, while harsh, low squawks express annoyance.
- Ask your child to pretend to be a dolphin and communicate with these sounds.

Read *There's a Dolphin in the Grand Canal* by John Bemelmans Marciano.

Hunting by Sound

Teaches about animals

- Explain to your child that some animals move around and hunt by sound rather than by sight.
- Explain that these animals listen for the faint rustling of moving prey. Many bats and whales find their way around by listening to echoes bounce off of objects. Still other animals listen for sounds from their own species as a way to find one another.
- Bring your child outside and sit together near a tree. Close your eyes and listen for birds or animals. Encourage your child to imagine what the birds or animals are trying to communicate with the sounds they are making.

Read *Sounds on the Farm* by Gail Donovan.

READ

CHAPTER 2

THE SENSE OF Sight

Which part of your body do you use to read a book, enjoy a rainbow, or see a snowball heading in your direction? Which part of your body do you use when you're sad and crying? Which part of your body do you use to see things both close and far away?

The activities in this chapter will explore the eyes, how they are used, and how the sense of sight adds enjoyment and learning to life.

Interesting Facts About Eyes, Sight, and Seeing

▶ It's impossible to sneeze with your eyes open.
▶ Women blink twice as much as men.
▶ If you go blind in one eye you only lose about one-fifth of your vision but all of your sense of depth.
▶ Our eyes are the same size from birth, but our nose and ears never stop growing.
▶ The average human being blinks his or her eyes 6,205,000 times each year.
▶ The entire length of all the eyelashes shed by a human in a lifetime is more than 98 feet (30 m).
▶ A frog can push its eyeballs back into the roof of its mouth to help move food down its throat.
▶ Dogs can see yellow and blue, but cannot distinguish red from green.

69

- Fish have eyes on the sides of their heads, helping them to see in almost every direction.
- Some animals have an extra set of eyes, called eyespots. They are fake eyes that can't see, but other animals can see them. What are these eyespots for? They protect animals from their predators!

Do these actions while you recite the following poem about what eyes can do:

An Eye Poem by Jackie Silberg
Look up, (look to the ceiling)
Look down, (look to the floor)
Look all around. (move your head back and forth)
Go blink, blink, blink (blink your eyes)
And shut them tight. (shut eyes tightly)
Give a yawn, (yawn)
And say "good night."

Sing the following song that celebrates the joy of sight:

Oh My Eyes by Jackie Silberg
(Tune: Did You Ever See a Lassie?)
Oh, my eyes can see the springtime, the springtime, the springtime.
Oh, my eyes can see the springtime, the trees are so green!
The grass and the flowers, the sunshine and showers,
Oh, my eyes can see the springtime, a beautiful sight!

Words That Describe Sight

Teaches vocabulary

- This is a wonderful language activity that helps children better understand the importance of their eyes.
- Ask your child to think of words that describe the different ways eyes look at things, including glaring, peering, gazing, staring, peeking, and so on, and then act out each way.
- Use these words in sentences, such as *gazing* at the sky and *peeking* over a fence.

Read *Look Again!* by Tana Hoban.

Eye Muscles

Teaches concentration

- Tell your child to hold his head straight and to look straight in front of him.
- Then, without moving his head, tell him to look at something in the room that will require him to move his eyes.
- Ask, "How did you get your eyes to move?"
- Explain that eye muscles move eyes from side to side, up and down, and around without moving the head.
- Ask your child to try moving his eyes each of those different ways. Ask, "Can you feel your eye muscles moving your eyes?"

Read *Look Up, Look Down* by Tana Hoban.

Let's Make an Eye

Teaches imagination

- Using a permanent marker, draw an iris and a pupil on the front of an inflated balloon.
- Give this "balloon eye" to your child so she can see that the pupil and the iris are in the front of the eye.
- Ask this "balloon eye puppet" questions about what it can see. "Do you see that pretty white cloud? Look, there's a rainbow!"

Read *Arthur's Eyes* by Marc Brown.

The Pupil

Teaches observation skills

GROUP GAME
- Talk about the pupil in the eye and explain that it gets larger to let in light when it is dark, and becomes smaller when there is a lot of light.
- Each child works with a partner.
- Turn off the lights and close the blinds to make the room dark.
- Ask the children to look at their partners' pupils when you turn the lights back on. They will be able to see the pupil change from large to small.

Read *The Eye Book* by Dr. Seuss.

Learning Games

The Blinking Game

Teaches about following directions

- The eye is almost the size of a ping-pong ball and sits in a little hollow area in the skull known as the eye socket. The front part of the eye is protected by the eyelid. Eyelids help to keep eyes clean and moist by opening and shutting several times a minute. This is called blinking, and it is both a voluntary and involuntary action. You can blink whenever you want to, but blinking also occurs when you are not thinking about it.
- With your child, sing a familiar song and each time you stop singing, blink your eyes together.

Read *Winking, Blinking, Wiggling, and Waggling* by Brian Moses.

Expressive Eyes

Teaches about emotions

- Ask:
  - Can you make your eyes look happy?
  - Can you make your eyes look sad?
  - Can you make your eyes look angry?
  - Can you make your eyes look silly?
  - Look in magazines for pictures of faces with happy, sad, angry, and silly eyes.

Read *Baby Senses Sight* by Susanna Beaumont.

Making Eyes

Teaches about the parts of the eye

- Draw an outline of an eye on a piece of poster board.
- Cut out a white oval and a small black circle from construction paper.
- Help your child glue the white oval on the poster board inside the outline of an eye.
- Help her cut out a large circle in her eye color.
- Ask her to glue the small black circle (pupil) onto the circle that is her eye color and then glue this onto the white oval.
- Now ask her to color in the eyelashes, eyebrows, and any other decorations she chooses to make.

Read *Look Closer* by Peter Ziebel.

My Eyes

Teaches eye movements

- Teach this rhyme to your child and then recite it together.

Here are my eyes. (point to your eyes)
One, two.
I can wink, (wink)
So can you.

When my eyes are open, (open eyes wide)
I can see the light.
When my eyes are closed, (close eyes)
It is dark as night.

Read *Look! Look! Look!* by Tana Hoban.

Different Words for Eyes

Teaches about languages

- Teach your child the word for eye in different languages:
  - in Spanish it is *el ojo*
  - in French it is *l'oeil*
  - in Italian it is *l' occhio*
- Make up a sentence about the eye and substitute the word for eye in a different language. For example, Say, "Here is my *ojo*," and point to your eye, or say, "My oeil is very important," and point to your eye.

Read *The Eye Book* by Dr. Seuss.

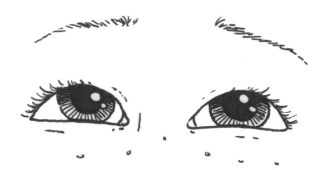

Different Colored Eyes

Teaches counting

GROUP GAME

▶ Ask the children which eye color they think most children in the group have.

▶ Pass around a small mirror and let each child look closely at the color of his or her eyes.

▶ On a chart, write each child's name and next to it the color of his or her eyes.

▶ Count the number of each color and announce whether the children were correct in their thinking.

▶ Count the colors for the boys and for the girls. Are they the same?

Read *Brown Bear, Brown Bear, What Do You See?* by Bill Martin, Jr.

Names	Eye Color				
	Brown	**Black**	**Blue**	**Hazel**	**Green**

Family Eye Color

Teaches observation skills

- On a piece of poster board, make a list of members of your child's family. Include aunts, uncles, grandparents, and even pets.
- Write the name of each person or animal, and next to each name draw an eye.
- When she discovers what color eyes each person or pet has, she colors in the eye next the person's name with the correct color.
- When the chart is completed, look at the chart to see which color is predominant.
- Remember, some people might have two eyes of different colors. In that case, draw two eyes next to that name and color each one appropriately.

Read *Goggles!* by Ezra Jack Keats.

Mom	👁	Grandpa	👁
Dad	👁	Aunt Pat	👁
Sally	👁	Uncle Dave	👁
Nicholas	👁	Trixie Cat	👁
Grandma	👁	Duke Dog	👁

Reflections

Teaches vocabulary

- Hold up a mirror, look into it, and say, "I can see my reflection in this mirror. It's a picture of my face!"
- Ask your child, "Would you like to see your reflection?"
- Give him the mirror so he can look at his reflection.
- Ask him to look at his eyes, nose, and tongue.

Read *My Mirror* by Kay Davis.

Self-Portrait

Teaches observation skills

- Ask your child to draw a picture of herself while looking in a mirror.
- Talk with her about the parts of her body that she can see.
- If she has any marks such as boo-boos on her body, point them out. Young children love talking about their boo-boos!

Read *Look! Look! Look!* by Tana Hoban.

The Eye Doctor

Teaches about letters

GROUP GAME

▶ Talk about the different kinds of doctors. The children will enjoy saying the word "ophthalmologist" or "optometrist."

▶ Make an eye chart using letters in various sizes.

▶ Select a child to be the doctor, and ask her to point to the letters on the chart.

▶ Let the other children say the letters, first using both of their eyes and then covering one eye at a time.

Read *Open Your Eyes: Discover Your Sense of Sight* by Vicki Cobb.

Glasses

Teaches sensitivity to the importance of eyes

▶ Cut out magazine pictures of people wearing glasses and paste them on a poster board.

▶ Talk about the pictures.

▶ Ask:
  ▶ Why do people wear glasses?
  ▶ Do glasses change the way people look?
  ▶ Does everyone look the same in glasses?

▶ Talk about how people wear glasses to see better, to protect their eyes while playing sports, and so on.

- Explain that when someone is farsighted he can see things clearly in the distance, but has trouble seeing things that are close up; when someone is nearsighted he can see things that are close up, but has difficulty seeing things at a distance.
- Make a list of ways to keep your eyes safe.
- Have your child draw a pair of glasses and decorate them.

Read *Magenta Gets Glasses!* by Deborah Reber.

Our Eyes Are Important

Teaches about understanding people who are blind

GROUP GAME
- The object of this activity is to walk around the room without using the sense of sight.
- Each child needs a partner.
- One child closes his eyes or wears a blindfold, and the other child (the leader) helps steer the blindfolded child away from danger.
- The blindfolded child holds the leader's arm.
- After a short while, the children switch roles. This activity helps children understand the importance of eyesight.

Read *Sights and Sounds: The Very Special Senses* by Charles E. Kupchella.

Understanding Braille

Teaches tactile skills

- Tell your child that people who are blind cannot see, but they can read with Braille.
- The Braille alphabet was invented by Louis Braille.
- Braille is a set of raised dots in different arrangements that represent letters and can be read with the fingers. It is used by people who are blind or whose eyesight is impaired.
- Put dots of glue or paste on a piece of paper. When it dries, there should be little bumps.
- Invite your child to feel the bumps to experience what Braille feels like.

Read *The Secret Code* by Dana Meachen Rau.

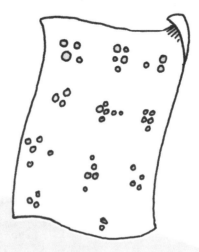

Watching Sign Language

Teaches about languages

▶ Look for situations when there will be someone using sign language. This might be a performance at a school for the deaf or a presentation that is interpreted with sign language.

▶ Talk with your child about what she might do if she could not hear anything. Explain how sign language would enable her to see someone "talk" with his hands.

▶ Learn a few basic signs and teach a song singing the words and using sign language at the same time.

Read *Pick Me Up! Fun Songs for Learning Signs* by Sign2Me.

Two Fingers From One

Teaches observation skills

▶ Have your child hold one index finger in front of his eyes.

▶ Have your child slowly bring his finger close to his eyes, keeping both eyes open.

▶ Your child will see the illusion of this finger turning into two fingers.

▶ Eyes can do amazing things!

Read *Sight* by Kay Woodward.

The Corner of Your Eye

Teaches visual awareness

- Ask your child to stare straight ahead without moving her eyes. This is very hard to do and will take some practice.
- Walk toward her from behind her back. Ask her to tell you when she sees you entering her field of vision.
- This demonstrates lateral peripheral vision.
- Another way to teach about peripheral vision is to hold a pencil above your child's head. Move the pencil downward and ask her to tell you when it comes into her field of vision.
- This game shows how we see out of the corners of our eyes.

Read *The Eye Book* by Dr. Seuss.

Two-Eye Game

Teaches about perception

- This is a fun game that shows how each eye sees the same image differently.
- Look at a picture on the wall from 20 or 30 feet away.
- Close one eye and hold up your arm to line up your finger with the picture, focusing on a specific part of the picture or one edge of the picture.
- Without moving your finger or your head, close the open eye and open the closed eye. The picture you are looking at will appear to move to the side and your finger will no longer be lined up with it.

Read *It Looked Like Spilt Milk* by Charles G. Shaw.

One Eye or Two?

Teaches the importance of both eyes

- Have your child hold a pencil in each hand and stretch his arms out straight.
- Ask him to close one eye and try to touch the ends of the pencils together.
- Now ask him to try it with both eyes open.
- Using both eyes makes this easier because each eye looks at the image from a different angle, giving better depth perception.
- You can also try this experiment with fingers!

Read *Look! Look! Look*! by Tana Hoban.

Drop It!

Teaches estimating skills

- You will need coins or buttons and a paper cup for this game.
- Sit at a table across from your child.
- Put a paper cup on the table in front of you and two feet away from your child.
- Ask your child to close one eye. Hold a coin in the air above the cup.
- Ask him to say, "Drop it!" when he thinks that your hand is lined up so that the coin will fall into the cup when you release it.
- When he says, "Drop it," drop the coin; see if it falls into the cup.
- Try it again having your child use both eyes. Try it several ways with the cup closer and farther away.
- Talk about the differences.
- Ask, "Does the coin drop into the cup more often when you use two eyes?"
- Ask, "Does the coin drop into the cup more often when the cup is closer to you?"

Read *Why the Frog Has Big Eyes* by Betsy Franco.

READ

Open, Shut Them

Teaches about following directions

▶ Invite your child to recite the following poem and make the suggested motions with her eyes.

Open, Shut Them adapted by Jackie Silberg
Open, shut them. (open and close your eyes)
Open, shut them. (open and close your eyes)
Look down to the ground. (move your eyes downward)
Open, shut them.
Open, shut them.
Circle round and round. (move your eyes around
*   in a circle)*
Look to the left and look to the right. (move your eyes
*   slowly left to right)*
Name three things you see. (let the child name
*   three things)*
Blink two eyes and wink one eye. (wink and blink eyes)
My eyes belong to me! (big smile)

Read *Open Your Eyes: Discover Your Sense of*
Sight by Vicki Cobb.

READ

Magnify Your Life

Teaches about looking very closely at things

- Using magnifying glasses, have your child take a closer look at her environment.
- Start with her clothes and her skin.
- Then she can look at everyday objects around her.

Read *You Can Use a Magnifying Glass* by Wiley Blevins.

Magnify Outside

Teaches about comparisons

- Go outside and use a magnifying glass to examine things in your outdoor environment; for example, snow, leaves, grass, or insects.
- Talk about how these things look different when you see them with and without a magnifying glass.

Read *Miffy's Magnifying Glass* by Dick Bruna.

The Binocular Game

Teaches observation skills

- Give your child a pair of binoculars and let her look through them.
- Play this game outside, if possible.
- Suggest objects for her to look for with the binoculars, such as birds in the trees, the doorknob on a house, or flowers in the garden.
- Talk about how the binoculars make things look closer.
- Find something to look at that is very far away.

Read *Look Again!* by Tana Hoban.

Another Binocular Game

- Ask your child to use the binoculars to look for objects that are certain colors. For example, "Find something blue."
- When he finds something blue, ask him to tell you what it is and then let you look at it, too.
- Reverse roles in the game, and have your child tell you to find an object that is a particular color.
- **Note:** For this game and for The Binocular Game (see previous page), use real binoculars or make pretend binoculars by taping together two toilet tissue cardboard rolls. If desired, attach a string so the "binoculars" can be worn around the neck. **Safety Note:** Supervise closely if child wears the binoculars around his neck.

Read *The Colors of the Rainbow* by Jennifer Moore-Mallinos.

Color My World

Teaches vocabulary

- Cut an opening in the middle of a paper plate. The opening should be large enough to look through.
- Tape a piece of colored cellophane over the opening.
- Give the plate to your child and ask her to talk about how the room looks through the colored cellophane.

The Sense of Sight

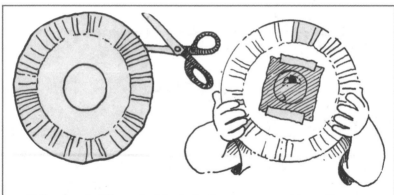

- Talk about different objects in the room and how they look different.
- Ask your child what you look like when she looks at you through the colored cellophane.

Read *See the Sea!: A Book About Colors* by Allia Zobel-Nolan.

Exploring Color

Teaches matching skills

- Ask a local paint store for sample color cards. If possible, obtain two of each card.
- These cards are wonderful to show the variety of colors available.
- Give the color cards to your child to match with similar colors in her surroundings.
- **Hint:** With young children, cut up the cards and put the same shade from each color card on two separate index cards, creating distinct color sample pairs.

Read *Eyes, Nose, Fingers, and Toes* by Judy Hindley.

Light and Dark

Teaches cognitive thinking

- Put equal amounts of water into three identical containers. Paper cups or drinking glasses work well.
- Put one drop of food coloring into one of the containers of water. Put two drops of the same food coloring into the next container and three drops of the same food coloring into the last container.
- Have your child arrange the colors from lightest to darkest.
- Try this with different colors of food coloring.

Read *Look Closer* by Peter Ziebel.

Mixing Colors

Teaches about colors

- Observing how colors change when they are mixed is a fascinating experience for young children.
- Mix yellow and blue food coloring in a bowl of water.
- Your child can see how these two colors make green.
- Ask your child what she thinks will happen when you mix red and blue. Ask, "What color will they make?"
- Try the same game with crayons.
- Encourage your child to experiment with color combinations.

Read *If You Take a Paintbrush: A Book About Colors* by Fulvio Testa.

Eyedropper Painting

Teaches fine motor skills

- Fill a shallow container with water.
- Color the water with food coloring. Let your child choose the colors.
- Encourage your child to fill an eyedropper with water and drop the water onto white construction paper.
- Let him try to make letters and shapes with the colored water.

Read *Sight* by Angela Royston.

Making a Mosaic

Teaches about colors

- Show your child what a mosaic looks like.
- With her, tear many different colors of paper into various shapes.
- Encourage her to glue the torn pieces of paper onto a large piece of paper to make her own mosaic.

Read *Teeny, Tiny Mouse: A Book About Colors* by Laura Leuck.

Glowing Mobile

Teaches about the stars and the moon

- Make a nighttime mobile with your child.
- Together, cut out stars and a moon shape from poster board.
- Paint them with paint that glows in the dark.
- Punch a hole in each piece and put a piece of yarn through it.
- Tie each piece of yarn to a hanger and hang the mobile from the ceiling.

Read *Twinkle, Twinkle, Little Star* by Iza Trapani.

READ

The Sense of Sight

Candy Eyes

Teaches creativity

- Make a candy eye with your child.
- Put a small gumdrop in the center of a candy lifesaver or other doughnut-shaped candy. Place a raisin in the middle of the gumdrop.
- Now you have an eye with a pupil and an iris.
- Eat the yummy eyes!

Read *Eyes* by Elizabeth Miles.

Find Color in Nature

Teaches observation skills

GROUP GAME
- Put several small strips of different colors of construction paper into a zipper-closure bag.
- Go outside.
- Ask a child to select one color strip from the bag.
- Everyone looks at the color of the construction paper strip and then tries to find something in nature that matches the color of the paper strip.
- This game takes a lot of visual discrimination skill.

Read *Color: A First Poem Book About Color* by Felicia Law.

Looking for Colors

Teaches thinking skills

- Select three colors and then go outside with your child to look for those colors.
- Look at trees, buildings, signs, cars, grass, and other things that are outside.
- As you see things that are the colors you have talked about, help your child write them on paper.
- When you get back inside, review the list.
- Discuss each word and talk about where you saw things of each color.

Read *The Color Kittens* by Margaret Wise Brown.

Looking for Song Pictures

Teaches matching skills

- Select a song your child enjoys singing, such as "The Wheels on the Bus."
- Ask him to look at magazines and catalogs for pictures that go with the song, such as a bus, a baby, children, windshield wipers, doors, windows, and wheels.
- Select several of the pictures and paste each onto a piece of construction paper. Now you have a "Wheels on the Bus" picture.
- Do this with other favorite songs.

Read *The Itsy Bitsy Spider* by Iza Trapani.

The Color of Eyes

Teaches about colors

- Fold a piece of white paper into four parts.
- On one part, ask your child to draw an eye.
- Give her a mirror and let her look at her eye and tell you its color.
- Ask her to color in her paper eye with her correct eye color.
- On the other three parts of the paper, ask her to draw things that are the same color as her eyes. For example, if her eyes are brown, she can draw a brown tree, a brown dog, and a brown shoe.

Read *What Does Bunny See?: A Book of Colors and Flowers* by Linda Sue Park.

Numbers in the Mirror

Teaches observation skills

- Write these numbers on the chalk board: 0, 1, 2, 3, 4, 5, 6, 7, 8, 9, and 10.
- Each number should be large and have lots of space around it.
- Ask your child to look at the numbers with a mirror.
- Ask, "Which numbers look the same in the mirror?" (0, 1, 8)
- Talk about why they look the same.

Read *Mirror, Mirror* by Allan Fowler.

Letters in the Mirror

Teaches observation skills

▸ Write these letters on a chalk board: A, B, C, D, E, F, G, H, I, J, K, L, M, N, O, P, Q, R, S, and T.

▸ Each letter should be large and have lots of space around it.

▸ Ask your child to look at the letters with a mirror.

▸ Ask, "Which letters look the same in the mirror?" (A, H, I, M, O, T)

▸ Ask, "Why do they look the same?"

Read *Otto: The Story of a Mirror*
by Ali Bahrampour.

Talking Stick

Teaches about taking turns

GROUP GAME

▸ One way to help children learn to take turns is to use a visual clue.

▸ Try using a "talking stick," a tradition with some Native Americans.

▸ Hold the stick while you speak and then pass it on when it is time for another person to speak.

▸ Explain to the children that only the person holding the stick is allowed to talk.

▸ **Note:** A talking stick can be made from anything. Use a stick from a tree or a toilet paper roll. If desired, decorate your talking stick.

Read *Look Again!* by Tana Hoban.

I Spy

Teaches listening skills

GROUP GAME

▶ This is a great game for developing observation skills.

▶ Pick an object that is visible to everyone, and keep it a secret.

▶ Give the children hints about the object and let them start guessing.

▶ The child who guesses the object gets to pick the next "I spy" object.

Read *I Spy Little Animals* by Jean Marzollo.

I Spy Shapes

Teaches observation skills

GROUP GAME

▶ Play "I Spy" with shapes.

▶ Say to the children, "I spy something round." When someone guesses the answer, he takes the next turn.

▶ Add triangles and squares to the game.

▶ **Note:** Younger children might need help with this game.

Read *Why the Frog Has Big Eyes* by Betsy Franco.

Treasure Hunt Fun

Teaches cognitive skills

▶ Hide five small objects, such as blocks, small toys, or cars, around the room.

▶ Send your child on a treasure hunt to see if she can find the objects.

▶ When all five have been found, play the game again, this time letting your child hide them so you can find them.

Read *Close, Closer, Closest*
by Shelly Rotner and Richard Olivo.

Looking for a Treasure

Teaches about following directions

GROUP GAME

- Plan a treasure hunt for the children. Walk with them to each stop on the treasure hunt. For example:
  - Give one child a yellow card with a picture of a car.
  - Walk to the toy car, and there will be another yellow card with a picture of a door.
  - Walk to the door, and there will be a yellow card with a picture of a chair.
  - The children find the chair that has a yellow card with another picture on it.
  - At the end of the search, there should be a treasure waiting, such as a new toy or book.
- Depending on the age of the children, make this a long or short treasure hunt.
- This is an excellent cognitive game and also develops visual acuity.
- **Note:** Use Post-Its for treasure hunt cards.

Read *The Treasure Hunt Book* by Klutz.

What's in the Bottle?

Teaches visual acuity

- You will need a clear plastic water or soda bottle.
- Place an assortment of small objects, such as crayons, buttons, beads, paper clips, and other objects in the bottle.
- Fill the bottle almost to the top with salt. Replace the lid and tape it securely.
- As your child rotates the bottle, the objects will come into view.
- Encourage him to talk about what he sees and describe the objects.

Read *Have You Seen My Cat?* by Eric Carle.

See Your Friends

Teaches vocabulary

GROUP GAME
- Ask each child to find a partner.
- Each pair of children looks at each other and describes what the other child looks like.
- Help the children with the descriptions.
- The children describe an aspect of the other child—the color of her eyes, hair, what she is wearing, and so on.
- This is a good game for developing visual awareness.

Read *The Colors of the Rainbow* by Jennifer Moore-Mallinos.

Who Is Missing?

Teaches observation skills

GROUP GAME

- Have the children sit in a circle and close their eyes.
- Silently, pick one child to hide in a designated area of the room that is out of sight of the rest of the children.
- Ask the children to open their eyes and look around to see who is missing.
- If necessary, give clues such as, "This person is wearing red today."

Read *I Spy Little Animals* by Jean Marzollo.

Close and Far

Teaches observation skills

- Draw two pictures of the same object, one small and one large.
- For example, draw a large airplane and a small airplane.
- Ask, "Which one is close and which one is far away?"
- Go outside with your child and look for an airplane in the sky. Ask your child, "Is it close or far away?"

Read *Estrellas Cercanas Y Lejanas / Stars Close and Far* by Robin Defter.

Watch for the Button

Teaches concentration skills

- Ask the children to sit in a circle. Select one child to sit in the middle of the circle.
- The children sitting around the circle pass a button from hand to hand behind their backs.
- The child in the middle uses his eyes to figure out who has the button.
- When he thinks he knows who has the button, he calls out that child's name.
- When he finds the button, he moves to the outer circle, and the child who had the button moves into the middle of the circle.

Read *What Does Bunny See?: A Book of Colors and Flowers* by Linda Sue Park.

Different Faces

Teaches imagination and creativity

- Glue a photograph of your child to a piece of paper.
- Go through magazines and newspapers with your child and cut out pictures of people, animals, and cartoon characters.
- Cut off the heads of these pictures and place them over the head of your child's photograph to see how she would look with a different head.
- Do the opposite and place bodies of people, animals, or cartoon characters over your child's photograph and see how she would look with a different body.
- This game can get very funny, especially if you mix things up a bit. For example, put a kitten or a clown body on a photograph of your child's head.

Read *Look Closer* by Peter Ziebel.

What Do You See?

Teaches observation skills

- Read the book *Brown Bear, Brown Bear, What Do You See?* by Bill Martin Jr.
- Read the book again and substitute your child's name for "brown bear."
- Ask him to respond with things he sees in the room. For example: "Michael, Michael, what do you see?" He responds, "I see a picture smiling at me."

Read *Look! Look! Look!* by Tana Hoban.

Matching Pictures

Teaches creativity

- Find action pictures in magazines and cut them in half vertically. Put the halves in two piles.
- Let your child select a picture from one of the piles.
- Ask her to imagine what the other half of the picture might look like. Then, let her find the picture from the other pile that goes with the picture she selected first.

Read *The Eye Book* by Dr. Seuss.

Do You Remember?

Teaches thinking skills

- Put five objects, such as a crayon, a block, a teaspoon, a toothbrush, and a bar of soap in front of you.
- Pick up each object and say its name.
- Cover the objects.
- Lift the cover and ask your child to look at the objects for five seconds. Replace the cover and ask him to tell you the objects he saw.
- Remove the cover again and see what objects, if any, were forgotten.
- Ask questions. "What makes it easy to remember the objects?" "Were they brightly colored?" "Were you familiar with some of them?" "How do our eyes help us remember?"

Read *Look Closer* by Peter Ziebel.

Eyes for Reading

Teaches literacy skills

- As you read a book, point to the words to encourage your child to follow along and begin to focus on printed materials.
- Play eye games with the book you are reading. Ask your child to look for certain pictures on a page.

Read *Beverly Billingsly Borrows a Book* by Alexander Stadler.

Fun With a Flashlight

Teaches thinking skills

- Place several objects such as a cup, a stuffed animal, block, and ball in a row along a wall.
- Turn off the light and make the room as dark as possible.
- Sit with your child across the room from the objects.
- Name an object for her to find and ask her to shine the flashlight on that object.
- Take turns holding the flashlight and finding objects.

Read *Look! Look! Look!* by Tana Hoban.

Sun and Shade

Teaches observation skills

- Go for a walk with your child on a sunny day.
- Look for shady places.
- Together, observe how the buildings and trees create the shade.
- Notice how your eyes adjust to the light in sunny spots and to the dark in shady spots.
- Have your child move from one shady spot to another by hopping, jumping, or tiptoeing.
- Ask, "Does sitting in the shade feel different from sitting in the sun?"

Read *Sight* by Angela Royston.

READ

Playing With Shadows

Teaches about shadows

- Go outside on a sunny day and look at your shadow.
- Encourage your child to make her shadow change. It can be big, tall, short, wide or small.
- Try to make different shapes with your shadow.
- Draw an outline of your child's shadow with chalk.

Read *My Shadow* by Robert Louis Stevenson.

Looking at Stars

Teaches awareness of the universe

- After dark, sit outside with your child and look at the stars.
- Watch for blinking stars.
- Talk about the stars and how very far away they are.
- Look for an airplane flying in the sky.
- Say star poems, such as the one that follows, and sing star songs such as "Twinkle, Twinkle, Little Star."

Star light, star bright,
First star I see tonight,
I wish I may, I wish I might
Have the wish I wish tonight

Read *Twinkle, Twinkle, Little Star* by Iza Trapani.

Describing a Leaf

Teaches about nature

- Using the sense of sight only, help your child describe various leaves.
- Describe the color. Ask, "Does it have veins?" "Does it have points on it?" "Does it have fuzz on it?" "Does the leaf have jagged edges?"
- This is challenging to do without touching the leaves.
- A good song to go along with this game is "Conversation With a Tree" by Jackie Silberg.

Read *"Miss Jackie's" I Love Children Songbook* by Jackie Silberg.

READ

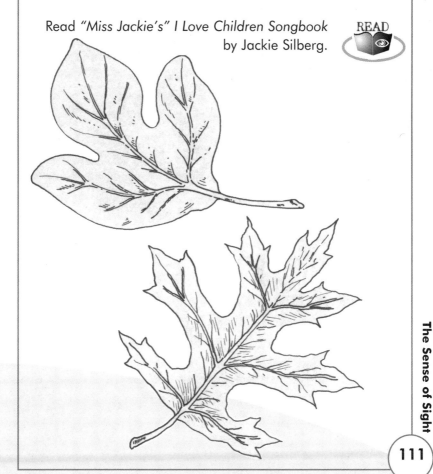

Looking at Clouds

Teaches imagination

▶ Go outside and sit down with your child. Look at the clouds in the sky.

▶ Talk about the different colors of the clouds. "Why are some clouds darker than others?"

▶ Talk about the different shapes of the clouds. Imagine what the shapes look like. "Do they look like sailboats, ice cream cones, or people?"

▶ Ask, "Can you see the sun behind the clouds?"

Read *It Looked Like Spilt Milk* by Charles G. Shaw.

Looking for Design

Teaches about shapes

- Using your eyes to look closely at things around you requires a lot of concentration.
- Ask your child to find shapes in the room. Look for squares, circles, and triangles.
- Look at boxes, doors, and charts.
- Practice looking closely at objects around you and you will find some interesting shapes and designs. For example, have your child look at windows and notice how the windowpanes are separated.
- Look closely at the floor, the ceiling, and the walls. Ask, "Do you see patterns or shapes?"
- This activity is wonderful for developing visual acuity.

Read *The Treasure Hunt* Book by Klutz.

Chameleon Eyes

Teaches thinking skills

- The eyes of the chameleon (a type of lizard) move independently and can see in two different directions at the same time.
- Ask, "Would you like to see in two directions at the same time? Why?"

Read *Jungle Animals* by Angela Royston.

Animal Eyes

Teaches about animals and how they see

- Some animals have eyes in front of their heads so they can focus clearly as they look for food. These animals, called predators, include owls, leopards, and lions.
- An animal that has eyes that face sideways is called a non-predator. Non-predators can see almost all the way around their bodies, offering lots of opportunity to spot a predator and run to safety. Non-predators include rabbits and raccoons.
- Look through nature magazines with your child and identify the kind of eyes that animals have, predator or non-predator.

Read *Eyes* by Elizabeth Miles.

Eagle Eyes

Teaches an awareness of environment

- A bald eagle can spot a mouse in a field from high in the sky.
- An eagle's keen eyesight allows it to focus on objects in front of it or to either side without moving its head.
- An eagle's eyesight is four times as sharp as the eyesight of a person with perfect vision.
- Ask your child, "What can you see without moving your head?"

Read *Look Once, Look Again: Animal Eyes* by David M. Schwartz.

Scorpion Eyes

Teaches creative thinking

- A scorpion can have as many as 12 eyes.
- Ask:
  - If you had 12 eyes, where would they be?
  - If you had eyes on your feet, what would they see?
  - If you had eyes on your back, what would they see?

Read *Scorpions: The Sneaky Stingers* by Allison Lassieur.

Compound Eyes

Teaches cognitive skills

- Imagine having eyes all over your body! Eyes on your arms, on your feet, on the top of your head! Eyes everywhere!
- Butterflies can see up, down, forward, backward, and to the sides, all at the same time.
- Butterflies can see many, many colors—more colors than humans.
- Ask, "If you had eyes on your arms, what would you see?" "What would you see if you had eyes on your head, or eyes on your feet?"

Read *Sight* by Angela Royston.

Walking Through Africa

Teaches another language

▸ This is a Zulu chant about what one might see in parts of Africa.

Walking through Africa, what do I see?
I can see inyoka looking at me.
Walking through Africa, what do I see?
I can see ufudu looking at me.
Walking through Africa, what do I see?
I can see indlovu looking at me.
Walking through Africa, what do I see?
I can see ikhozi looking at me.

Notes

inyoka (een-yoh'-gkah) a snake
ufudu (oo-foo'-doo) a tortoise, /oo/ as in fool
indlovu (een-dloh'-voo) an elephant
ikhozi (ee-koh'-zee) an eagle

Read *Juba This and Juba That: 100 African-American Games for Children* by Dr. Darlene Hopson.

READ

CHAPTER 3

THE SENSE OF Touch

The sense of touch is the most primitive and pervasive sense. While the other four senses—sight, hearing, smell, and taste—are located in specific, discrete parts of the body, your sense of touch originates in the bottom layer of your skin called the *dermis*. Every bit of skin on your body, including your nails, is used for touching. The nerve endings in the skin send signals to the brain, the brain analyzes the signals, and you feel the effects of touch.

The activities in this chapter explore hands and skin, how you use them to touch and feel things, and how the sense of touch adds enjoyment and learning to life.

Interesting Facts About Animals and the Sense of Touch

▶ A cat's whiskers act as sensitive feelers. These special hairs stick out from the cat's cheeks and chin and above its eyes. Cats are active at night, and their whiskers help them feel their way around in the dark. Whiskers are so sensitive they can detect the slightest change in a breeze.

▶ Animals that sleep during the day and are active at night are called *nocturnal* animals. These animals have a well developed sense of touch that provides information about their surroundings. Nocturnal animals include bats, leopards, possums, tigers, and wolves.

▶ Animals also use their sense of touch to communicate and to find food. Touch receptors are often concentrated around certain body parts, such as whiskers on cats.

Recite the following poem and do the actions.

Eye winker, (gently touch eyelid)
Tom tinker, (gently touch the other)
Nose dropper, (gently touch nose)
Mouth eater, (gently touch mouth)
Chin chopper, (gently touch chin)
Guzzle whopper. (tickle belly)

Sing familiar songs about hands, including:
▶ "If You're Happy and You Know It"
▶ "Where Is Thumbkin?"
▶ "He's Got the Whole World in His Hands"

Exploring Hands

Teaches body awareness

- Ask your child to use the fingers of one hand to touch her other hand. If she closes her eyes as she does this, she will be able to concentrate better.
- Ask your child to decide if the back of her hand is softer than the palm of her hand.
- Ask her to notice how smooth her fingernails feel.
- Have your child open her eyes and look very closely at the hand she just touched.
- Notice the knuckle wrinkles and veins on the back of the hand, the lines on the palm, the fingerprint whorls.

Read *Find Out by Touching* by Paul Showers.

What Can Hands Do?

Teaches thinking skills

- Ask your child to tell you the different things his hands can do.
- Start the conversation by saying, "My hands can feel things. What can your hands do?" Suggestions include:
- Scratch your head. How does it feel?
- Clap your hands. How does it feel?
- Pick up food. How does it feel?
- As he tells you what his hands can do, help him write his answers on a piece of paper.

Read *Here Are My Hands* by Bill Martin, Jr. and
John Archambault.

The Sense of Touch

No Hands

Teaches patience

- While sitting down, ask your child to put her hands on her head or in her lap. See how long she can go without using her hands.
- If appropriate, time this game with a clock.

Read *Hand, Hand, Fingers, Thumb* by Al Perkins.

Hand Greetings

Teaches social skills

- One way to greet another person is to shake his or her hand.
- With your child, demonstrate different ways to shake someone's hand, including shaking gently and shaking vigorously.
- Act out each way of greeting someone.
- Of course, there is always the "high five."

Read *The Chocolate Touch* by Patrick Skene Catling.

Different Words for Hand

Teaches about languages

- The word for hand:
  - in Spanish is *la mano*.
  - in French is *la main*.
  - in Italian is *la mano*.
- Ask your child to make up sentences about the hand, substituting a different language word for *hand*. For example, say, "Here is my *mano*," and point to your hand, or say, "My *main* can feel" and point to your hand.

Read *The Kissing Hand* by Audrey Penn.

Touching

Teaches body awareness

- Ask your child to focus on what her hands are doing as she does the actions and says the following.

Touching by Jackie Silberg
I can touch my hair and eyes.
I can stand up straight and rise.
I can touch my ears and nose,
And sit back down and touch my toes.

Read *Touch* by Susanna Beaumont.

What Child Is This?

Teaches thinking skills

GROUP GAME

- Sit in a circle.
- Select one child and blindfold him. Ask all of the children to stay silent.
- Quietly lead the blindfolded child to another child and, without anyone talking, direct the blindfolded child to touch the face of that child.
- Ask the blindfolded child to guess the name of the person whose face he is touching.

Read *Night-Night, Baby: A Touch-and-Feel Book* by Elizabeth Hathon.

A Matching Game

Teaches matching skills

- Display pairs of several items, such as two spoons, two forks, two crayons, and so on.
- Put one of each item into a large paper sack.
- Put the matching item on a table in front of you.
- Ask your child to find one item in the bag that matches the item you have selected. "Can you find the fork?"
- Be sure she puts her hand into the sack *without looking* and finds the match by feel.

Read *I Can Tell by Touching* by Carolyn Otto.

Touch the Room

Teaches classification skills

▶ Ask your child to walk around the room and look for different textures to touch.
▶ After he has familiarized himself with how things in the room feel, ask him to look around the room and touch something soft. Ask him how many soft things can he find.
▶ Ask him to continue looking for things that are *hard, bumpy, cold, warm,* and *smooth.*

Read *Touch and Feel: Home* by Dorling Kindersley Publishing.

Feeling Different Sensations

Teaches thinking skills

▶ Ask your child to try the following sensations:
  ▶ Place her index fingers together and push. This will create a sense of pressure on each hand.
  ▶ Brush her index fingers on each other and feel the gentle, stroking touch.
  ▶ Touch an ice cube with her fingers. How does her body feel after touching the cold ice cube?
  ▶ Dip her fingers into a bowl of warm water. How does her body feel after touching the warm water?

Read *I Can Tell by Touching* by Carolyn Otto.

Spiders

Teaches about spiders

▸ Spiders learn about the world by feeling vibrations in the air.

▸ Their eyesight is poor; they can only see light, dark, and basic shapes.

▸ When something is causing a spider web to move, the spider can tell by the vibration of the air what is causing the movement.

▸ Shake a piece of paper in front of your child's hand and let him feel the air move. Now hold the paper still and ask him to feel the difference.

Read *Spiders* by Gail Gibbons.

Where's the Touch?

Teaches body awareness

- Blindfold your child.
- Use a ballpoint pen or washable marker to touch a spot on her skin.
- Gently, leave a small pen mark on her skin.
- While she is still blindfolded, give her a pen of a different color and ask her to touch the point that you just touched.
- How close is the child's guess to the actual point that you touched?
- This is great fun for children and makes them aware of their eyesight as well as of their sense of touch.

READ

Read *Touch* by Maria Ruis.

Foot Touching

Teaches language skills

- Remove your child's shoes.
- Have him walk in mud, walk in sand, walk on rocks, and walk in water.
- Ask him to describe how each material felt; ask him to compare the feelings.

Read *The Barefoot Mailman* by Theodore Pratt.

READ

Another Foot Game

Teaches vocabulary

- Line the bottom of three shoeboxes with materials of three different textures, such as sandpaper, cotton, and velvet.
- Have your child take off her shoes and socks and feel the inside of each box with her bare feet.
- Talk about how each one feels, using descriptive words such as *hard, soft, smooth, scratchy,* and so on.

Read *Whose Feet?* by Nina Hess.

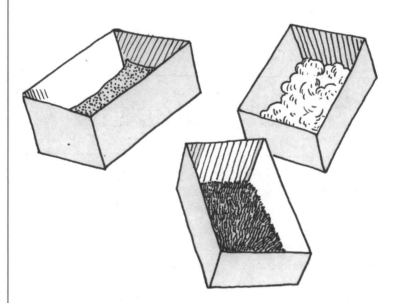

Feet on Hands

Teaches coordination

- Trace your handprints on a variety of materials, such as wood, carpet, linoleum, fake fur, silk, and other materials that have interesting textures.
- Cut out the handprints.
- Securely attach these handprints to the floor.
- Ask your child to walk barefoot across the tracks.
- Make the handprints turn, go backward, forward, and zigzag.
- Try it again with your child crawling on the handprints.

Read *Happy Hands & Feet* by Cindy Mitchell.

Walking on Bubbles

Teaches motor skills

- Tape a sheet of bubble wrap securely to the floor.
- Have your child take off his shoes and walk across the bubble wrap.
- Encourage your child to try walking in different ways, such as tiptoeing, stomping, running, hopping, and walking on heels.
- Ask your child to try walking without popping any of the bubbles.

Read *What Can You Feel With Your Feet?* by Hertha Klugman.

Pop the Bubbles

Teaches coordination

- Blowing bubbles and feeling them pop in the air is lots of fun!
- You can also cut out pieces of bubble wrap and let your child pop the bubbles.
- With bubble wrap, show your child how to squeeze the bubbles to pop them, or put the bubble wrap on a table so she can push down on the bubbles to pop them.
- Children enjoy this tactile experience.

Read *Pop!: A Book About Bubbles* by Kimberly Brubaker Bradley.

Touching Place

Teaches about the senses

- Set up a "Touching Place" with interesting objects to touch, such as sandpaper, sand, fur, felt, satin, cotton, wool, rocks, foil, an orange or a lemon, and other objects with unique textures.
- This "Touching Place" offers your child a chance to experience different sensations of touch.

Read *The Touch Book* by Jane Belk Moncure.

A Touch Poem

▶ With your child, say the following poem about the sense of touch and do the actions:

Touch your shoulders,
Touch your knees,
Touch your hands behind you,
Please.

Touch your elbows,
Touch your toes,
Touch your hair,
And touch your nose!

Touch the wall,
Touch the floor,
Touch the table,
Touch the door.

Read *The Sweet Touch*
by Lorna and Lecia Balian.

READ

The Sense of Touch

What Do You Feel?

Teaches concentration

- Ask your child if it is possible to determine whether an object is cold, hot, smooth, or rough by the way it feels on our skin.
- Ask your child to close his eyes or put on a blindfold.
- Touch an item, such as an apple (smooth), a rock (rough), or a piece of ice (cold), to his hand or fingers and ask him to tell you how it feels.

Read *Touch and Feel: Home* by Dorling Kindersley Publishing.

Touching Skin

Teaches body awareness

- The skin is the organ of the body that is used for touching. Every bit of skin on our bodies, including our nails, is used for touching.
- Different parts of our bodies—hands, feet, and fingers—are more sensitive to touch than others.
- Take an object with an irregular surface—a wet sponge works well—and touch it to your child's elbow or knee. Touch it anywhere but the hand.
- Then, touch the sponge to her fingertips. The fingertips will be more sensitive than the other parts of the body.

Read *Fuzzy Fuzzy Fuzzy!: A Touch, Skritch, & Tickle Book* by Sandra Boynton.

Body Sensitivity

Teaches thinking skills

- This game helps children realize how things feel on different parts of the body.
- Gather several different objects with interesting shapes, sizes, and textures, such as a tennis ball, an eraser, a rock, a sponge, a pinecone, a sponge, a wooden spoon, and a piece of velvet.
- Ask your child to close her eyes and touch the items to different parts of her body, such as the back of her neck, her elbow, and her foot.
- Ask:
  - How hard was it to identify the object?
  - Would it be easier to identify it with your fingers?
- Talk about how easy it is to identify an object using the fingers compared to using another part of the body.

Read *Is It Rough? Is It Smooth? Is It Shiny?* by Tana Hoban.

Feeling Different Temperatures

Teaches about warm and cool

- Gently warm everyday objects, such as a towel, a small toy, or a stuffed animal.
- Let your child feel the objects.
- Cool the objects in a refrigerator.
- Let your child feel the objects again.
- Compare the differences.

Read *Look, Listen, Taste, Touch, and Smell: Learning About Your Five Senses* by Pam Hill Nettleton.

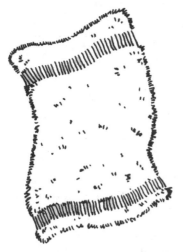

Feely Chart

Teaches vocabulary

- Write descriptive words across the top of a piece of paper. Include words like *hot, cold, wet, dry, hard, soft, rough,* and *smooth.*
- Gather several objects to show your child.
- Pick up an object, such as an ice cube. Ask your child if it feels *hot* or *cold.* Is it *wet* or *dry*?
- Keep asking these questions and write the word *ice cube* under the words that describe it.
- Continue with the other everyday objects.

Read *Fuzzy Fuzzy Fuzzy!: A Touch, Skritch, & Tickle Book* by Sandra Boynton.

Feely Chart

	Hot	Cold	Wet	Dry	Hard	Soft	Rough	Smooth
Object								
Ice Cube								
Hair brush								
Jello								

Changing Sand

Teaches vocabulary

- Cover a table with newspaper.
- Fill a deep tray such as a dishpan or a deep baking pan with sand and place it on the table.
- Put a cup of water next to the sand tray.
- Let your child slowly pour the cup of water into the sand.
- As the sand gets wet and the texture changes, talk about what is happening and encourage your child to describe how it feels. Use *mushy*, *cold*, and other descriptive words.

Read *I Can Tell by Touching* by Carolyn Otto.

Shaving Cream Fun

Teaches creativity and imagination

- You will need a table that you can get wet.
- Wet a paper towel and rub it all over the table to get it wet.
- Put a small blob of shaving cream onto the table.
- Encourage your child to cover the entire table with the shaving cream, using his hands to make designs or anything else in the shaving cream.
- Ask him to describe the texture of the shaving cream.
- **Note:** An apron is recommended for this activity.

Read *Learning How to Use the Five Senses: See, Hear, Taste, Touch, Smell* by Elizabeth Mechem Fuller.

Touching Clay

Teaches fine motor skills

- Provide clay or playdough for your child.
- Encourage her to mold the clay or playdough into different objects.
- Ask her to describe how she is using her hands to mold the playdough or clay.
- This activity lets her express herself creatively with her hands.

Read *The Little Hands Big Fun Craft Book* by Judy Press.

Slime

Teaches about thick and thin

- Children love to play with Slime. It is a fun sensory activity.
- To make Slime, mix cornstarch with a little water and stir well. Continue to add water until you get the right consistency; it should be fairly stiff when rolled in the hand, but melts through the fingers when not rolling. If it gets too thick, just add more water; if it is too thin, add more cornstarch.
- To make it colorful, add food coloring.
- Store Slime in the refrigerator after each use.
- Encourage your child to use her hands to explore the properties of Slime.
- Ask her to describe how Slime feels.

Read *Pure Slime: 50 Incredible Ways to Make Slime Using Household Substances* by Brian Rohrig.

Fingerpaint With Textures

Teaches fine motor skills

- Let your child fingerpaint with materials that have a unique texture, such as liquid starch or whipped soapsuds.
- Add powdered tempera for color.
- Add sawdust or other materials that have different textures.
- This is a wonderful way to feel textures and to internalize the concept of how they feel.

Read *My Fingers Are for Touching* by Jane Belk Moncure.

Painting on Textures

Teaches thinking skills

- Provide tempera paint, paintbrushes, and painting surfaces that have different textures, such as corrugated paper, sandpaper, and Styrofoam.
- Encourage your child to paint on these textured surfaces.
- Ask her to describe the similarities and the differences in painting on papers with different textures.

Read *Texture* by Karen Bryant-Mole.

Interesting Textures

Teaches vocabulary

- Add different materials, such as sand, salt, coffee grounds, or cornmeal to tempera paint to give it interesting texture.
- Provide paintbrushes and paper.
- Let your child paint with these textures and describe how they look and feel.

Read *Fuzzy Yellow Ducklings: Fold-Out Fun With Textures, Colors, Shapes, Animals* by Matthew Van Fleet.

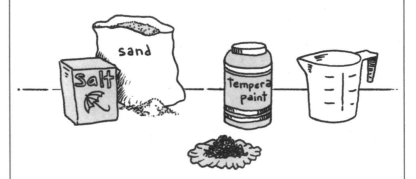

Feely Book

Teaches vocabulary

- Make a feely book by labeling each page with a texture word, such as *rough*, *bumpy*, *smooth*, *soft*, or other appropriate words.
- **Note:** Use a blank book or create your own book by stapling pieces of paper together and then covering the staples with duct tape.
- Tape or glue appropriate textured material to each page. For example, glue a piece of sandpaper to the page labeled *rough*.
- Add a literacy component by making up a story to go with the book.

Read *My Fuzzy Safari Babies: A Book to Touch & Feel* by Tad Hills.

smooth

My Hands Can Touch

Teaches thinking skills

- Trace your child's hand on white paper.
- Ask him to name five things he likes to touch.
- Write the five things he names on the fingers of the hand.
- Ask him to draw pictures of things he likes to touch around the handprint, or to cut out pictures from magazines of things he likes to touch and glue them around the handprint.

Read *Here Are My Hands* by Bill Martin, Jr. and John Archambault.

Poster Board Hands

Teaches artistic expression

- Trace your child's hand on poster board and cut out the hand shape.
- Give her a variety of items to glue on the hand, each finger, or each fingernail. Suggestions include sandpaper, cotton balls, a piece of fur, a piece of velvet, textured fabric, and sequins.
- Ask her to describe the textures of the hand she has created.

Read *The Mudpies Activity Book: Recipes for Invention* by Nancy Blakey.

141

Texture Picture

Teaches about creativity

- Make a picture using different textured fabric and other objects, such as buttons, cotton balls, and other objects.
- Cut out a circle from felt for the body. Use other materials to make the arms and legs. Use cotton balls for the eyes.
- Give your child a variety of materials to use on her picture.
- Ask her to describe the textures in her picture.

Read *Textures* by Karen Bryant-Mole.

Crayon Rubbing

Teaches fine motor skills

- Gather several different shapes of leaves.
- Invite your child to feel the texture of the leaves.
- Help your child make crayon rubbings by placing a sheet of thin white paper over one or more of the leaves and rubbing the paper with the side of the crayon.
- Talk with your child about the texture of the leaves that created the picture.

Read *Learning How to Use the Five Senses: See, Hear, Taste, Touch, Smell* by Elizabeth Mechem Fuller.

Natural Texture Names

- Help your child write his name on a paper plate.
- Go for a walk and look for items to glue onto the letters of his name, such as small pebbles, grass, and twigs.
- When you think you have enough, come inside and glue the items onto the letters that you have drawn on the paper plate.
- Now your child can show off his beautiful name made with textures from nature.

Read *My Fingers Are for Touching*
by Jane Belk Moncure.

The Sense of Touch

143

Wallpaper Books

Teaches about designs

▶ Old wallpaper books are wonderful resources for feeling textures. Some stores will give you books they no longer use.
▶ Turn to one page in the wallpaper book.
▶ Ask your child to look at the design on that page and describe it without touching it.
▶ Then ask her to feel the design and describe how it feels.

Read *Is It Rough? Is It Smooth? Is It Shiny?* by Tana Hoban.

Apples and Oranges

Teaches counting skills

▶ Put three apples and three oranges into a large paper or opaque plastic bag.
▶ Ask your child to tell you how many apples are in the bag and how many oranges are in the bag, using only her sense of touch.

Read *Clifford Counts Bubbles* by Norman Bridwell.

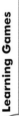

Feeling Fruit

Teaches cognitive skills

- Place an orange, an apple, and a banana in separate paper or opaque plastic bags.
- Ask your child to close his eyes and identify the fruit in each bag by feeling the outside of the bag. No peeking!
- Ask him how he determined what was in each bag.

Read *Find Out by Touching* by Paul Showers.

Bag Mysteries

Teaches vocabulary

- Fill three plastic bags with different textured materials; for example, sand, small stones, and playdough.
- Let your child feel each bag and tell you how each feels.
- It is important to help her identify the vocabulary to use, such as *squishy, hard, soft, smooth,* and so on.

Read *Is It Rough? Is It Smooth? Is It Shiny?* by Tana Hoban.

Unwrap the Present

Teaches fine motor skills

▶ Wrap several small toys in a variety of papers, such as foil, plastic, and fabrics.

▶ As your child unwraps each item, talk about how the wrapping feels. Use words like *soft, slick, rough,* and *smooth*.

Read *The Little Hands Big Fun Craft Book* by Judy Press.

What Am I Touching?

Teaches listening skills

GROUP GAME

▶ Place objects that have a unique texture, such as a sponge, a rock, and a piece of velvet, on a tray.

▶ Talk with your child about each object and let him hold and feel each one.

▶ Put the tray out of sight and tell him that you are going to describe one of the objects.

▶ For example, say, "I am feeling something that is hard and rough," and ask him to guess which object you are describing.

▶ Continue, describing the other objects.

Read *Look, Listen, Taste, Touch, and Smell: Learning About Your Five Senses* by Pam Hill Nettleton.

Learning Games

A Feeling Description

Teaches language skills

GROUP GAME

▶ Place several familiar objects, such as a ball, a spoon, a rock, and a leaf, inside a paper bag.

▶ Let the children see what you are putting in the bag.

▶ Ask one of the children to put her hand into the bag and pick one of the objects. Ask her to keep her hand in the bag so the object is not visible to the other children.

▶ Ask her to use only her sense of touch to describe what she is holding to the other children. Ask, is it *long, flat, round, soft,* and so on.

▶ The child who guesses the object gets to pick the next object.

▶ **Variation:** Ask another child to find an object that is larger or smaller than the first object, using only the sense of touch.

Read *Feeling Your Way: Discover Your Sense of Touch* by Vicki Cobb.

Outside Touching

Teaches vocabulary

- Go outside to touch different things.
- As you touch them, help your child find words to describe how each item feels.
- You can touch leaves, flowers, grass, rocks, branches, pebbles, and more.
- Some of the words you can use are *smooth, rough, prickly, fuzzy, soft, hard,* and *sticky.*

Read *Touch* by Andreu Llamas.

Fun in the Kitchen

Teaches thinking skills

- Select three or four kitchen tools; for example, tongs, a baster, a wire whisk, and a melon ball scoop.
- Talk with your child about how each tool is used as he holds that tool. You can act out how to use each of the tools.
- Put all of the tools into a paper grocery bag.
- Let your child put his hand in the bag and feel one of the tools.
- See if he can tell you which one it is.
- **Note:** If possible, use one of the tools to cook with. You could whip some eggs or scoop some melon.

Read *The Chocolate Touch* by Patrick Skene Catling.

The Butterfly

Teaches creative movement

GROUP GAME

▶ Sit in a circle and choose one child to be a butterfly.

▶ The butterfly waves her arms as she "flies" outside the circle.

▶ When she "lands," by gently touching someone's back, that person becomes the butterfly. The other children will have to be ready to notice the butterfly's gentle touch.

▶ Say the following poem while the butterfly is flying.

The Butterfly

Butterfly, butterfly, fly away
On this lovely summer day.
Fly up in the sky so blue,
And when you land, it will be on (name of child).

Read *The Very Hungry Caterpillar*
by Eric Carle.

Jigsaw Puzzles

Teaches cognitive skills

- Put together a jigsaw puzzle using only the sense of touch.
- Get a simple children's puzzle with four to six pieces. The best are those with a raised rim around the border.
- Put the puzzle together with your child.
- Now try putting it together without looking at the pieces. Show her how to feel each piece before putting it in the puzzle.

Read *My Fingers Are for Touching* by Jane Belk Moncure.

Feel the Shape

Teaches about shapes

- From heavy cardboard or tagboard, cut several shapes, such as a circle, a square, a triangle, and any other shapes your child will recognize.
- Ask your child to close his eyes. Ask him to feel the shape and to guess what shape it is by using his sense of touch.
- **Variation:** Make this more challenging by cutting the same shapes in different sizes.

Read *I Can Tell by Touching* by Carolyn Otto.

Touching Toys With a Song

Teaches memory skills

GROUP GAME

▸ Sit with the children in a circle.

▸ Put several toys in the middle of the circle and ask the children to name each toy.

▸ Now put all of the toys in a large box or bag and let the children touch them one by one as the box or bag is passed around the circle.

▸ As each child touches one of the toys, all the children sing the following to the tune of "Frere Jacques":

What's your toy, what's your toy?
Say its name, say its name.

▸ The child who is touching the toy tells the name of the toy and pulls it out of the box or bag.

Read *Hand Clap! "Miss Mary Mack" and 42 Other Hand Clapping Games for Kids* by Sara Bernstein.

How Does This Feel?

Teaches thinking skills

▶ Glue different materials or items to index cards. Cover the entire index card with one of the following—buttons, ribbons, leaves, twigs, bubble wrap, or Styrofoam bits.

▶ Put each card in a separate paper bag.

▶ Ask your child to reach into one of the bags and identify the surface she is touching.

Read *Whose Back Is Bumpy?* by Kate Davis.

Complicated Matching

Teaches about shapes

▶ Cut out two of the same shape from poster board or cardstock, one large and one small.

▶ Cut additional shapes, a large one and a small one of each.

▶ Ask your child to close her eyes and try to match the two shapes that are the same—the large one and the small one.

▶ This takes cognitive thinking and very careful feeling.

Read *Touch and Feel Buggy Buddies: Shapes* by Ant Parker.

Feeling Socks

Teaches memory skills

- Obtain four socks and mark each with a numeral from 1 to 4.
- In each sock, put an object to feel and identify, such as a wooden block, a coin, a pencil, or a crayon.
- Give your child a piece of paper divided into four parts. Number each section.
- As your child feels each sock, without removing the object, he draws a picture of what he is feeling.
- When he finishes the drawings, empty the socks and see if he recognized what he felt.

Read *The Little Hands Big Fun Craft Book* by Judy Press.

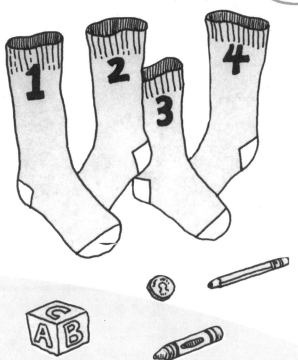

Seven Up—#1

Teaches fun

GROUP GAME

- ▶ Choose seven children from the group.
- ▶ Ask the other children to sit down, close their eyes, and put their heads down.
- ▶ **Note:** Be sure there is room to move around each child.
- ▶ Ask the first seven children to walk quietly around the children that have their heads down. Each of the seven children touches one person. The children who were touched—seven who had their heads down—put one hand in the air while staying seated with their heads down.
- ▶ The first seven children move away from the group and say, "Heads up, seven up."
- ▶ Each child who was tapped gets one chance to guess which of the seven children touched him or her.
- ▶ If a child guesses correctly, he or she changes places with that child. If the child guesses incorrectly, he or she stays in the first group of seven children.
- ▶ This is too much fun to play just once!

Read *Look, Listen, Taste, Touch, and Smell: Learning About Your Five Senses* by Pam Hill Nettleton.

READ

Seven Up—#2

Teaches fun

GROUP GAME

▶ Ask all of the children to sit down and put their heads down.

▶ **Note:** Be sure there is room to move around each child.

▶ Ask everyone to hold up one hand and extend the thumb on that hand.

▶ Very quietly, choose one child to be "IT."

▶ IT moves quietly around and touches the thumbs of six people. When a child's thumb is touched, he moves quietly to the front of the room.

▶ When all six children are standing together at the front of the room with IT, IT yells, "Seven up!"

▶ All of the children raise their heads and try to guess which of the seven people is IT.

Read *The Mudpies Activity Book: Recipes for Invention* by Nancy Blakey.

CHAPTER 4

THE SENSE OF Smell

The sense of smell plays an important role in our sense of well-being and our quality of life. We smell with our noses. When we breathe in the air around us, smells go into our noses. Almost everything has its own smell, including flowers, pies, perfume, and skunks! Your sense of smell brings you into harmony with nature, warns you of danger, and sharpens your awareness of people, places, and things.

The activities in this chapter will explore the nose, how you use it to smell, and how the sense of smell adds enjoyment and learning to life.

Interesting Facts About the Nose, Smells, and Smelling

▶ If your nose is working at peak performance, you can tell the difference between 4000 and 10,000 smells!

▶ As you get older, your ability to smell fades. Children are more likely to have a better sense of smell than their parents or grandparents.

▶ Feet smell because they perspire, causing bacteria to form, which causes the bad smell. Wash your feet and wear clean socks to keep your feet smelling fresh! It is a good idea to change your shoes every day and to give each pair of shoes 24 hours to air out.

Interesting Facts About Animals and Their Noses

- Dogs have 1 million smell cells per nostril. Their smell cells are 100 times larger than those of human beings.

- Bloodhounds have the keenest sense of smell. They can recognize a person or animal by its scent. Bloodhounds learn to track a person by sniffing an article of clothing or an item handled by that person. They find that person by following the scent trail. Bloodhounds are good at finding lost people and missing pets.

- Jaguars are nocturnal animals that rely on their sense of smell to find prey in the dark.

- Giant pandas usually live alone; they use their keen sense of smell to find each other in thick bamboo forests.

- The rhinoceros has poor eyesight. It relies on its strong sense of smell to find other rhinos, even when they are far away.

- Gazelles use their keen sense of smell to tell when a predator is sneaking up on them.

- Elephants use their long noses, called "trunks," to smell the air for danger that might be nearby.

Sing the following "Smell Song" to the tune of "Do Your Ears Hang Low?"

Does your nose hang low?
Does it wiggle to and fro?
Can you give it a big squeeze?
Can you make it give a sneeze?
Can you throw it o'er your shoulder
Like a Continental Soldier?
Does your nose hang low?

Smell and Taste Together

Teaches about taste

- Most people think only of the tongue when they think about tasting. But you cannot taste without help from the nose!
- Smelling and tasting go together because the smell of food allows us to taste the food more completely.
- Invite your child to take a bite of food and think about how it tastes. Now, ask your child to pinch his nose and take another bite. Ask if there is a difference.
- Aren't we lucky to have a nose!

Read *How Do We Taste and Smell?*
by Carol Ballard.

Nose, Nose

Teaches vocabulary

- Use your sense of smell to describe and compare the spices mentioned in this poem.

Nose, nose, jolly red nose,
Who gave thee that jolly red nose?
Nutmeg and ginger, cinnamon and cloves,
That's what gave me this jolly red nose.

Read *Smell* by Maria Rius.

Does Smell Change the Taste?

Teaches about taste

- Put three pieces of pineapple and one slice of lemon on a paper plate. Put a toothpick in each piece.
- Hold the piece of lemon under your child's nose. Make sure it is very close to her nose.
- Have her eat a piece of pineapple while smelling the lemon.
- Now hold the lemon a little farther away from her nose while she eats another piece of pineapple. Ask, "Does the pineapple taste the same or different?"
- Put the lemon slice back on the plate. Have your child eat the last piece of pineapple. What does it taste like?

READ

Read *Tasting Things* by Allan Fowler.

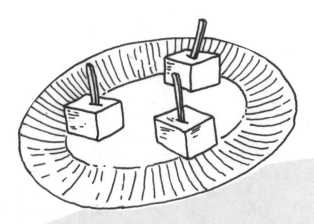

Smelling Herbs

Teaches memory skills

- Select two or three herbs with very different odors. These are easy to find in the supermarket. Suggestions include tarragon, parsley, dill, sage, and chives.
- Gently rub an herb on your child's wrist and ask him to smell it.
- Do the same with other herbs and ask him to smell them.
- Now, rub your own wrist with one of the herbs and help your child try to remember and identify the smell.

Read *Breathtaking Noses* by Hanna Machotka.

Different Words for Nose

Teaches about languages

- Learn the word for *nose* in different languages:
  - in Spanish it is *la nariz*
  - in French it is *le nez*
  - in Italian it is *il naso*
- Make up a sentence about the nose and substitute a different language word for *nose*.

For example, say, "Here is my *naso*," and point to your nose, or say, "My *nez* is very important," and point to your nose.

Read *The Nose Book* by Al Perkins.

T-Shirt Experiment

Teaches an awareness of smell

▶ Explain to your child that each person has his or her own smell.

▶ Ask your child to wear a clean T-shirt for a few hours and then to take off the shirt and mix it up with other unworn shirts.

▶ Put a blindfold on the child.

▶ Using just his sense of smell, ask him to find the shirt he wore. No touching!

Read *What's That Smell?* by Janelle Cherrington.

How Smell Protects Us

Teaches about safety

- Light a match. Blow it out.
- Ask your child what she smells and what that smell tells her.
- Talk about how smells warn us of danger. For example, smoke from a fire, the rotten smell of spoiled foods, and the smell of gas leaking from a stove.
- Encourage her to think of other smells that protect us by serving as a warning sign that something is wrong.
- Talk about how our sense of smell keeps us safe. Ask, "How can it warn us of danger? If you smell smoke, what should you do?"

Read *The Senses I Smell With My Nose* by Joan Mills.

Air Fresheners

Teaches about smells

- Insert cloves into a whole orange to make a homemade air freshener.
- Tie a ribbon around the orange, tying a loop at the top. Use the loop to hang the orange.
- Or, wrap mesh netting around the orange and then stick in the cloves. This makes the color more interesting.
- It smells wonderful!

Read *Clifford Follows His Nose* by Norman Bridwell.

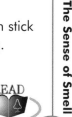

Making a Flower

Teaches fine motor skills

- Glue a cupcake liner onto a piece of construction paper.
- Glue several cotton balls into the middle of the cupcake liner. (Offer to help your child, if necessary.)
- Let him draw green stems on the sides of the liner so it looks like a flower.
- Let him spray the cotton balls with a perfume atomizer. (Dilute the perfume and supervise closely.)
- Now he has lovely, fragrant flowers!

Read *Follow Your Nose: Discover Your Sense of Smell* by Vicki Cobb.

Candle Smells

Teaches thinking skills

- Take a trip to a candle store.
- Have your child smell all of the aromas and see how many she can identify.
- Make a list of the different smells.
- Try to identify other products that have that same smell. For example, cinnamon is also found in candy, peach is found in a fruit, jasmine is found in a flower, and mint is also found in a plant.

Read *What's That Smell?* by Janelle Cherrington.

Acting Out Smells

Teaches imagination

GROUP GAME

- Talk about acting out the way you look when you smell things. For example, if you were smelling flowers, how would your face look?
- Act out facial and other reactions to certain smells, such as flowers, smoke, perfume, rotten eggs, and smelly feet.
- Ask the children to guess what you are smelling.
- Switch parts and let the children take turns acting out how they look when they smell things.

Read *Learning How to Use the Five Senses* by Elizabeth Mechem Fuller.

To Market, to Market

Teaches about fruits and vegetables

- Visit a market.
- Enjoy the wonderful smells of fruits, vegetables, and flowers.
- Show your child how to smell a fruit to see if it is ripe.
- Say the following poem:

  To market, to market
  To buy a fat pig.
  Home again, home again,
  Jiggity, jig.

Read *You Can't Smell a Flower With Your Ear* by Joanna Cole.

Smelly Walk

Teaches vocabulary

- Walk around any room or go outside.
- Ask your child to describe what she smells.
- Write down her words.
- Talk about what she smelled.
- Ask her if the smells were *good, bad, sweet,* and so on.

Read *David Smells!* by David Shannon.

Smells We Like and Smells We Don't Like

Teaches thinking skills

GROUP GAME
- With the children, make a list of things that smell good to them. Ideas might include flowers, perfumes, soaps, chocolate chip cookies, freshly mowed grass, and so on.
- Then make a list of things that smell unpleasant or dangerous. Ideas might include garlic, smoke, rotten food, and sour milk.
- Ask whether everyone agrees on what smells good and bad.

Read *Learning How to Use the Five Senses* by Elizabeth Mechem Fuller.

Smells to Remember

Teaches memory skills

- Smells often trigger memories.
- Ask your child:
  - If you smell a piece of cake, what does that remind you of?
  - If you smell perfume, what or who do you think of?
  - If you smell freshly cut grass, what do you think of?
- Talk about how smells remind us of things that are both pleasant and unpleasant.

Read *Smell* by Mandy Suhr.

Fit the Smell

Teaches vocabulary

▶ Say certain words that describe smells, such as *fruity*, *sweet*, *delicious*, *sour*, *rotten*, and *yucky*.
▶ Ask your child what might make those smells.
▶ Make a list of what he says.

Read *Grandma, Tell Me a Story*
by Lynn Floyd Wright.

Where's the Smell?

Teaches thinking skills

▶ Make a list of places, items, or events, such as the kitchen, the beach, a swimming pool, a barbecue, a fireworks display, and so on.
▶ With your child, make a list of the smells associated with each place, item, or event.
▶ Ask your child for additional suggestions of places, items, or events that have specific smells.
▶ Add these to the list.

Read *Smell* by Maria Ruis.

Pictures of Smells

Teaches literacy skills

- Take Fit the Smell (page 169) one step further.
- Make a chart on paper or poster board. Write the name of the smell on the left side with a related picture next to it.
- For example, print *sweet* and put a picture of a cake next to the word. Print *fruity* and put a picture of a lemon next to it, *spicy* and put a picture of a cinnamon stick next to it, or *clean* and put a picture of a bar of soap next to it.
- Ask your child to look through magazines and cut out pictures that fit a particular smell.
- Select pictures and paste them on the chart where they belong.

Read *I Smell Christmas* by Mercer Mayer.

Scratch and Sniff

Teaches about smells

- Show your child three different scratch-and-sniff stickers.
- Talk about the picture on each sticker.
- Place the three stickers on a piece of paper.
- Blindfold your child and help him scratch one of the stickers and then ask him to smell it.
- Take off the blindfold and see if he identified the correct odor.
- Suggest that he draw a picture of what he smelled next to the sticker.

Read *The Stinky Easter Egg* by Chris Tougas.

I Like to Smell Picture

Teaches fine motor skills

▸ Encourage your child to cut out pictures from magazines and catalogs of things she likes to smell.

▸ Ask her to paste the pictures onto a piece of construction paper.

▸ Encourage her to talk about the pictures and use words to describe the smells, such as *sweet, strong, clean,* and so on.

Read *Little Bunny Follows His Nose* by Katherine Howard.

Sweet Picture

Teaches fine motor skills

▸ Give your child drawing paper and crayons or markers.

▸ Ask her to draw a picture of something sweet on the paper.

▸ Help her cover the picture she has drawn with glue.

▸ Then help her sprinkle Jell-O® powder over the glue. Let it dry.

▸ When it is dry, she can scratch and smell her "sweet" picture.

Read *Bite-Sized Science* by John H. Falk.

Smell the Picture

Teaches about colors

- Sprinkle a small amount of dry Kool-Aid mix onto a piece of paper.
- Using a variety of colors will make the sight and smell more interesting.
- Ask your child to use his index finger and draw a design on the Kool-Aid mix.
- Help him spray water from a spray bottle onto the paper. Let it dry.
- Smell the picture.

Read *Follow Your Nose: Discover Your Sense of Smell* by Vicki Cobb.

Does It Smell?

Teaches about differences

- Put three small containers on a table. Film canisters work well.
- Fill each with a different clear liquid, such as water, vinegar, and alcohol.
- **Note:** The above is an adult-only step.
- Ask your child to tell you which containers smell and which ones do not smell.

Read *Smelling Things* by Allan Fowler.

Can You Name the Smell?

- Tell your child that she is going to use her sense of smell.
- Ask her, "What do we use to smell?" (our noses)
- Ask her to close her eyes. Place an orange and then a lemon under her nose.
- Ask her if she can recognize the two smells.
- After she has guessed, correctly or incorrectly, she can open her eyes.
- Ask her to look around the room and name things that have a smell. For example, crayons, paints, soap, and other objects that have a distinct smell.

Read *Who's Making That Smell?* by Jenny Tyler and Philip Hawthorn.

Sniff and Smell

Teaches matching skills

- You will need clean, plastic spice jars or similar size containers.
- Create smell jars by filling each jar with something that has a distinctive odor, such as lemon, vinegar, and peppermint.
- Place a small amount of the material in a jar.
- **Note:** Put cotton balls inside the jars to prevent spills but still allow sniffing.
- Cover the jars with paper so it is not possible to see what is inside each jar.
- Ask your child to smell each jar and identify the scent.
- Mix up the order of the jars and see if your child can still identify the scents.
- **Variation:** Create sets of smell bottles and ask your child to identify the sets using her sense of smell only.

READ

Read *Smell* by Maria Ruis.

What Do You Need to Smell?

Teaches about animals

▶ People use their noses to smell. Other animals use their tongues, their antennas, or even their feet to smell!

▶ No matter what kind of animal, a sense of smell requires three things:
 1. Something that smells.
 2. Something to smell with.
 3. A brain to identify the smell.

▶ With your child, discover how different animals smell things. For example, an elephant smells with its trunk, a butterfly smells with its antennae, and a squirrel smells with its nose.

Read *Breathtaking Noses* by Hanna Machotka.

Little Skunk's Hole

Teaches about following directions

▶ Skunks are capable of making a very foul smell!
▶ Sing this song about skunks to the tune of "Dixie."

Oh, I stuck my head in the little skunk's hole
And the little skunk said, "Well, bless my soul.
Take it out. Take it out.
Take it out. Remove it!"

Oh, I didn't take it out and the little skunk said,
"If you don't take it out,
You will wish you had.
Take it out! Take it out!"
Pheeew, I removed it.

▶ Ask your child what she thinks happened!

Read *Tanka Tanka Skunk!* by Steve Webb.

The Elephant

Teaches humor

▶ Enjoy the following poem about elephants, which have very long noses!

The elephant goes like this and that. (walk like an elephant on all fours)
He's very big and very fat. (hold your arms up high and out to the side)
He has no fingers and no toes, (point to your fingers and toes)
But, my, oh, my, what a nose! (point to your nose)

Read *The Story of Babar* by Jean de Brunhoff.

Animal Smell Game

Teaches imagination

GROUP GAME

▸ Put a different food in each of several zipper-closure, plastic bags.

▸ Select foods that have distinct odors, such as oranges, tuna fish, and bananas.

▸ Explain to the children that animals search for food by using their sense of smell.

▸ Ask the children to sit in a circle and close their eyes.

▸ Pass one of the plastic bags around and let each child smell what is in it.

▸ After the child has smelled the bag, ask him to say, "I am a (name of an animal) and I smell (name of smell)." Follow this with the animal sound. For example, "I am a tiger and I smell oranges. Grrr."

▸ **Note:** After the children have smelled the food, be sure to store it away properly or serve it for snack so that it is not wasted.

Read *Grandma, Tell Me a Story* by Lynn Floyd Wright.

READ

Animal Noses

Teaches about animals

- ▶ Cut out pictures of different animal noses.
- ▶ Show your child one of the noses and ask her to name the animal that the nose belongs to.
- ▶ Let her pretend to be each animal she identifies and pretend to smell something the animal would like. For example, a dog might like to smell a bone, a monkey might like to smell a banana, and a horse might like to smell oats.
- ▶ This game is a lot of fun, especially when pretending to be a pig.

Read *Breathtaking Noses* by Hanna Machotka.

CHAPTER 5

THE SENSE OF
Taste

The sense of taste is crucial to our good health. One reason taste and smell sensations are important is that they prepare your body for digesting food. For example, tasting and smelling food trigger your salivary glands and digestive juices. Without them, your stomach would not be ready for food, and you would have trouble digesting food and making good use of the nutrients you get from food.

Another reason why taste is crucial to your health is that it provides information about food. After even a tiny taste of some foods, it is possible to detect "off" flavors that may signal that the food has spoiled. You rely on your sense of taste to warn you about foods that may be dangerous to your health.

The activities in this chapter will explore the tongue, how you use it to taste, and how the sense of taste adds enjoyment and learning to life.

Interesting Facts About the Sense of Taste

▶ An American painted lady butterfly walks on her food to taste it.
▶ Butterflies, bees, and houseflies have taste receptors on their feet. These receptors have special cells that help them taste.

Sing the following "Tongue Song" to the tune of "Do Your Ears Hang Low?"

> *Does your tongue hang down?*
> *Can you wiggle it around?*
> *Can you move it side to side?*
> *Can you stop and make it hide?* (put it inside your mouth)
> *Can you throw it o'er your shoulder*
> *Like a Continental Soldier?*
> *Does your tongue hang down?*

Using Your Tongue

Teaches body awareness

- Ask your child, "Is it possible to eat an ice cream cone without your tongue?"
- Our tongue helps us do many things, including:
  - chew (pretend to chew)
  - swallow (pretend to swallow)
  - taste (pretend to taste something)
- Notice how the tongue makes each of these motions possible.
- Ask your child, "What else can a tongue do?"

Read *Eating the Alphabet* by Lois Ehlert.

Different Words for Tongue

Teaches about languages

- The word for tongue:
  - in Spanish is *la lengua.*
  - in French is *la langue.*
  - in Italian is *la lingua.*
- Make up sentences about the tongue, substituting a different language word for *tongue.* For example, Say, "Here is my *langue,*" and point to your tongue, or say, "My *lingua* is very important," and point to your tongue.

Read *Your Tongue Can Tell: Discover Your Sense of Taste* by Vicki Cobb.

Tongue Bumps

Teaches about comparisons

- The bumps on the tongue are called *papillae*; inside each bump are hundreds of taste buds.
- Ask your child to stick out his tongue and look at the bumps on his tongue in a mirror.
- The tip of the tongue is best for tasting sweet things, the sides for sour. Saltiness is detected all over, and the taste buds at the back of the tongue detect bitter tastes.
- Touch the different parts of the tongue and name things that have tastes that are detected by each different part of the tongue—sweet, sour, salty, and bitter.

Read *Bear Wants More* by Karma Wilson.

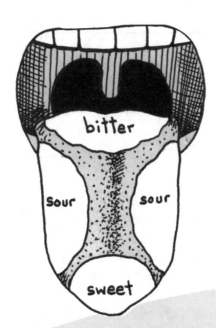

Sweet or Sour

Teaches about comparisons

▸ Partially fill one paper cup with lemon juice and a second paper cup with lemonade.
▸ Give your child a cotton swab, such as a Q-tip®, and ask her to dip it into the lemon juice and then touch the cotton swab to her tongue.
▸ Ask her to do the same with the lemonade.
▸ Talk about the differences between sweet and sour tastes.

Read *Good Enough to Eat: A Kids' Guide to Food and Nutrition* by Lizzy Rockwell.

Another Sweet-or-Sour Game

Teaches concentration skills

▸ This is similar to Sweet or Sour, above.
▸ Partially fill one paper cup with lemon juice and a second paper cup with a sweetened liquid.
▸ Give your child a cotton swab, such as a Q-tip®, and ask him to dip it into the lemon juice and then touch the cotton swab to different parts of his tongue.
▸ Ask him to do the same with the sweetened liquid.
▸ Talk about the differences in the taste. Is the taste stronger? Is the taste the same?

Read *If You Give a Mouse a Cookie* by Laura Joffe Numeroff.

What Taste Is This?

Teaches problem solving

▶ Put the following items on a paper plate: a pinch of salt, a lemon wedge, a pinch of sugar, and a taste of horseradish.

▶ Ask a child to taste each item and to identify it as *salty, sour, sweet,* or *bitter.*

▶ Between each taste, give her a piece of celery to chew to cleanse her mouth and get rid of any unpleasant taste.

Read *I Will Never NOT EVER Eat a Tomato* by Lauren Child.

Tasting Water

Teaches discovery about water

- Pour tap water, soda water, mineral water, and clear flavored waters in separate paper cups.
- Let your child taste each of the water samples.
- Discuss the differences in the tastes.

Read *Senses* by Angela Royston.

Let's Taste Red

Teaches about colors

- Have your child taste red foods, such as strawberries, raspberries, tomatoes, apples, rhubarb, red peppers, and red punch.
- Repeat with another color of foods.
- Plan a rainbow table of tastes with foods of many different colors.

Read *Your Tongue Can Tell: Discover Your Sense of Taste* by Vicki Cobb.

Apple Tasting

Teaches vocabulary

- ‣ Apples have many flavors, and each flavor is fun to taste!
- ‣ Select three different apples from varieties including Granny Smith, Red Delicious, Golden Delicious, Pink Lady, Jonathan, and Fuji.
- ‣ Cut each apple into four parts.
- ‣ Have your child taste a part of each apple and talk about the difference in the tastes. Some are sweet and some are sour.
- ‣ The textures are different too. Some are crunchy and some are softer to chew.
- ‣ If possible, go to a fruit stand or supermarket to find different varieties of apples.
- ‣ On the Jewish holiday, Rosh Hashanah, children dip apples in honey to wish for a sweet year.

Read *A Taste of Honey* by Nancy Elizabeth Wallace.

Let's Make a Smoothie

Teaches about combining foods

- Start by having your child taste a strawberry and a banana.
- Then mix 5 strawberries, half a banana, ½ cup of milk, 4 ounces of yogurt, and 4 ice cubes in a blender, and voila! You've got a smoothie!
- Ask which tastes are still identifiable in the blended smoothie.
- Ask, "Is one taste more prominent than the others?"

Read *Tasting Things* by Allan Fowler.

Chocolate

Teaches language skills

- Children in Mexico often drink chocolate with breakfast. They stir it with a special utensil called a *molinillo* (moh-lee-NEE-yoh), which is held upright between the palms and rotated back and forth in a spinning motion.
- Say the "Rima de Chocolate" before or after drinking chocolate milk or hot chocolate.
- While saying this rhyme, rub your palms together and pretend to stir the chocolate with a *molinillo*, repeating the verse faster and faster each time.
- If possible, use a molinillo to make chocolate milk or hot chocolate.

Read *The Chocolate Day* by Ann Herrick.

READ

Jellybean Fun

Teaches how the senses work together

- Sort jellybeans by flavor into small paper cups. Give your child one cup with one flavor of jellybeans in it.
- Put a blindfold on your child. Ask him to pinch his nose while he chews a jellybean and to guess the flavor of the jellybean he is eating.
- Now tell him to let go of his nose while he keeps the blindfold on, and then eat another jellybean from the same cup. Can he identify the taste now?
- Ask, "Why was it difficult to identify the flavor of the jellybean when you pinched your nose?"
- Our sense of smell and taste are connected!

Read *Peter's Party Senses: Taste* by Sue Sherliker.

Tasting in Space

Teaches fine motor skills

- Tell your child that she is going to pretend to be an astronaut and that she will be eating a meal in space.
- Pour half a box of pudding into a plastic, zipper-closure bag. Pour into a measuring cup enough milk to make half a box of pudding and help your child add it to the bag.
- Seal the bag very carefully. Let her squish the bag around with her hands, mixing the milk and the pudding.
- Cut a small hole in the corner of the bag and suggest that she suck out the pudding.
- Ask her, "Does pudding taste different in space?"

Read *Taste* by Maria Ruis.

Food Song Polka

Teaches vocabulary

- The following are the lyrics to "The Food Song Polka" by Jackie Silberg.
- Ask your child to name foods he has tasted when he hears them in the song.

Food Song Polka by Jackie Silberg
Capellini, fettucini, escargot, and bok choy.
Jambalaya and papaya, teriyaki, bok choy.
Herring, kippers, guacamole,
Kreplach, crumpets, ravioli,
Gyros, gumbo, sushi, curry, poi, bok choy.
Tacos, baklava, egg rolls,
French fries, rumaki, Sally Lunn.
Bratwurst, lasagna, wonton,
Chow mein, ceviche, crab rangoon.
Weiner schnitzel, salted pretzels, sauerkraut, and bok choy.
Moo goo gai pan, enchilada, sauerbraten, bok choy.
Herring, kippers, guacamole,
Kreplach, crumpets, ravioli,
Gyros, gumbo, sushi, curry, poi, bok choy.

- Try a food mentioned in the song that your child has never tasted.

Read *Bread and Jam for Frances* by Russell and Lillian Hoban.

Today Is Monday

Teaches the days of the week

- This popular children's song is perfect for talking about taste.
- After singing the song, talk about each of the different foods in the song and how each tastes.
- Categorize them into *salty, sweet, sour,* and *bitter.*

Today Is Monday
Today is Monday,
Today is Monday,
Monday wash day,
All you lively children
We sing the same to you.

Today is Tuesday,
Today is Tuesday,
Tuesday string beans,
Monday wash day,
All you lively children
We sing the same to you.

Today is Wednesday,
Today is Wednesday,
Wednesday soup,
Tuesday string beans,
Monday wash day,
All you lively children
We sing the same to you.

Today is Thursday,
Today is Thursday,
Thursday roast beef,
Wednesday soup,
Tuesday string beans,
Monday wash day,

All you lively children
We sing the same to you.

Today is Friday,
Today is Friday,
Friday fish,
Thursday roast beef,
Wednesday soup,
Tuesday string beans,
Monday wash day,
All you lively children
We sing the same to you.

Today is Saturday,
Today is Saturday,
Saturday pay day,
Friday fish,
Thursday roast beef,
Wednesday soup,
Tuesday string beans,
Monday wash day,
All you lively children
We sing the same to you.

Today is Sunday,
Today is Sunday,
Sunday church,
Saturday pay day,
Friday fish,
Thursday roast beef,
Wednesday soup,
Tuesday string beans,
Monday wash day,
All you lively children
We sing the same to you.

Read The Magic School Bus: Explores the
Senses **by Joanna Cole and Bruce Degen.**

Betty Botter

Teaches alliteration

▸ This tongue twister is all about *bitter* and *better* tastes.

▸ Ask whether your child can say it without getting tongue-tied.

Betty Botter

Betty Botter bought some butter,
But she said, "The butter's bitter.
It will make my batter bitter.
But a bit of better butter
Is sure to make my batter better."
So she bought a bit of butter
Better than her bitter butter,
And she put it in her batter
And the batter was not bitter.
So 'twas better Betty Botter
Bought a bit of better butter.

▸ After all that tongue exercise, try some bread and butter! Ask, "Is the butter *better* or *bitter?*"

Read *Your Tongue Can Tell: Discover Your Sense of Taste* by Vicki Cobb.

READ

Chocolate Chip Cookies

Teaches rhythm

▶ Enjoy the following poem about tasting chocolate chip cookies.

Chocolate Chip Cookies

Chocolate chip cookies, you gotta have more.
You can bake 'em in the oven, or buy 'em at the store.
But whatever you do, have 'em ready at my door,
And I'll love ya till I die.

They're made out of sugar and butter and flour.
You put 'em in the oven about a quarter hour,
But the thing that gives them their magic power
Is the chocolate chips inside.

Chocolate chip cookies, you gotta have more.
You can bake 'em in the oven, or buy 'em at the store.
But whatever you do, have 'em ready at my door,
And I'll love ya till I die.

You can't eat one, you can't eat two.
Once you start chewing, there's nothing to do,
But clean your plate, and eat the crumbs too.
Then go and find some more.

Chocolate chip cookies, you gotta have more.
You can bake 'em in the oven, or buy 'em at the store.
But whatever you do, have 'em ready at my door,
And I'll love ya till I die.

Now when I die, I don't want wings,
A golden halo or a harp that sings.
Give me a book, a fire, and someone that brings me
Chocolate chip cookies all day.

Chocolate chip cookies, you gotta have more.
You can bake 'em in the oven, or buy 'em at the store.
But whatever you do, have 'em ready at my door,
And I'll love ya till I die.

▶ Talk about how chocolate tastes. Name other foods with chocolate.

Read *Chocolate Chip Cookies* by Karen Wagner.

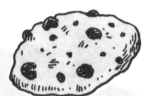

Taste Inventory— What's the Taste?

Teaches classification

- Make a chart from poster board or tagboard with *sweet, sour, bitter,* and *salty* written in a column down the left side of the chart.
- Look through magazines and catalogs to find pictures of food.
- Cut out several pictures of foods and put them into a basket.
- Pick out a picture and ask your child which taste category it belongs to. For example, a picture of gumdrops would go in the *sweet* category.
- Paste the gumdrop picture next to *sweet.*
- Continue with other pictures of food.
- Enhance the learning and fun of this game by providing samples of food to taste.

Read *The Popcorn Book* by Tomie dePaola.

READ

Taste Inventory	
sweet	
sour	
bitter	
salty	

Taste Picture Book

Teaches thinking skills

- Look through magazines and catalogs to find pictures of foods that have a *sweet* taste.
- Cut out the pictures and paste each one on a separate piece of construction paper.
- Write *sweet* at the top of each picture.
- Look for pictures of things that taste *sour, salty,* and *bitter.*
- Paste each one on a piece of construction paper and label the taste.
- Gather the pieces of construction paper, putting the pictures in each taste category together.
- Attach with metal rings or loops of yarn, creating your very own Taste Picture Book.

Read *Look, Listen, Taste, Touch, and Smell:* *Learning About Your Five Senses* by Pam Hill Nettleton.

Imagining Tastes

Teaches imagination

- Make up imaginary flavors for things in the environment!
- Ask your child about his favorite tastes, such as licorice, chocolate, pizza, and so on.
- Ask him to imagine that things he sees every day taste like his favorite tastes! He might imagine chocolate doors, licorice chairs, pizza windows, and more.
- This is great fun!

Read *The Gingerbread Boy* by Paul Galdone.

Name That Taste

Teaches language skills

GROUP GAME

▶ Sit in a circle with the children.

▶ Ask the first child to tell the others something she likes to taste.

▶ Continue with each child telling something he or she likes to taste.

▶ Start again with the first child and ask her to tell the others something that she does *not* like to taste and why she does not like it.

▶ This game is a great way to begin a discussion about taste!

Read *If You Give a Pig a Pancake*
by Laura Joffe Numeroff. READ

CHAPTER 6

THE
FIVE
Senses

Everyday life is filled with sensory experiences. It is easy to offer young children the opportunity to explore the world through their five senses. Encourage them to see, hear, smell, touch, and taste things in their environment.

The activities in this chapter will explore how the five senses add enjoyment and learning to life.

Interesting Facts About the Five Senses

▶ A chameleon's tongue is twice the length of its body.
▶ A chimpanzee can learn to recognize itself in a mirror, but a monkey cannot.
▶ About 10% of the world's population is left-handed.
▶ A person afflicted with *hexadectylism* has six fingers on one or both hands or six toes on one or both feet.
▶ The world's largest rodent is the *Capybara,* an Amazon water hog that looks like a guinea pig; it can weigh more than 100 pounds and makes a very loud noise.
▶ The world's smallest mammal is the bumblebee bat of Thailand, which weighs less than a penny and makes a very soft noise.
▶ The giant squid, usually found in the deep reaches of the oceans, has the largest eye of any animal.
▶ Butterflies taste with their feet.

Recite the following poems, and as you do, touch the part of the body that relates to each of the five senses.

Five Senses Poem by Jackie Silberg
Five little senses are a part of me,
My ears to hear and my eyes to see.
I taste with my mouth, and I smell with my nose.
And I touch with my hands and sometimes with my toes.

Here Are My Eyes by Jackie Silberg
Here are my eyes to look around.
Here are my ears to listen to a sound.
Here is my nose to smell something sweet.
Here is my mouth that likes to eat.

I'm Me
I have five fingers on each hand.
Ten toes on my two feet.
Two ears, two eyes, one nose, one mouth,
For tasting things so sweet.
My hands can clap, and snap, and tap,
And with my eyes I see.
My ears can hear, my nose can smell,
My mouth can say, "I'm me!"

Five Senses Game
(hearing, sight, touch, smell, taste)

Teaches about comparisons

- You will need two small containers with lids.
- Fill one container with sugar and one with salt.
- Ask your child to open each container, touch both the sugar and the salt, and then describe how each one feels.
- Ask him to smell each one and ask if they are the same or different.
- Ask, "Do they *look* the same or different?"
- Shake each container and listen to the sound.
- Taste each substance. Ask, "Do they taste the same or different?"
- Repeat this with any two substances that look similar and are safe to taste.

Read *My Five Senses* by Margaret Miller.

READ

What Can We Touch?
(hearing, sight)

Teaches thinking skills

- Ask your child, "What can we learn about the world by using our sense of touch?"
- Continue, asking other questions, such as:
  - Can you touch the moon or the stars? Which sense do you use to experience the moon or the stars?
  - Can you touch thunder? Which sense do you use to experience thunder?
  - Can you touch a cloud? Which sense do you use to experience a cloud?

READ

Read *Nature Spy* by Shelly Rotner and Ken Kreisler.

What Senses Do You Use?

(hearing, sight, touch, smell, taste)

Teaches observation skills

GROUP GAME

▶ Look through magazines and catalogs for pictures of ears, eyes, noses, mouths (including tongues), and hands.
▶ Cut the pictures out.
▶ Glue each picture on an index card.
▶ Let each child select a card and ask the child to say which sense the picture represents.
▶ Ask her what she does with that sense. For example, if she selects an index card with an eye, she can say that she uses her sense of sight to see clouds in the sky.
▶ If another child also picks a card with a picture of eyes, it will be interesting to hear what he says about how he uses the same sense in a different way.

Read *My Five Senses* by Aliki.

Which Sense?

(hearing, sight, touch, smell, taste)

Teaches thinking skills

GROUP GAME

▶ Find pictures of three different things: an animal (for example, a lion); an object (for example, a car); and a food (for example, a banana). Make sure all of the pictures are of things that are familiar to children.

▶ Hold up the picture of the animal (in this case, a lion).

▶ Ask the children these questions about a lion:
  ▶ Can you see a lion?
  ▶ Can you hear a lion?
  ▶ Can you smell a lion?
  ▶ Can you taste a lion?
  ▶ Can you touch a lion?

▶ This game makes for wonderful discussions!

▶ Continue, using the object (car) picture and the food (banana) picture.

Read *The Magic School Bus: Explores the Senses* by Joanna Cole and Bruce Degen.

READ

Name Five
(hearing, sight, touch, smell, taste)

Teaches memory skills

- This is a very good way to get a child's attention.
- Say the following words and do the actions described.

  My eyes are looking.
  My ears are listening.
  My nose is smelling.
  My mouth is closed.
  My hands are at my side.

- Repeat often. Soon your child will say them with you.

   Read *My Five Senses* by Margaret Miller.

Body Part Senses
(hearing, touch, smell, taste)

Teaches about body awareness

- Name a body part and ask questions about it.
- The following example uses the toe.
  - Can you see with your toe?
  - Can you hear with your toe?
  - Can you smell with your toe?
  - Can you taste with your toe?
  - Can you feel with your toe?
- Continue with other parts of the body.

   Read *My Five Senses* by Judy Nayer.

Five Senses for the Hand

(hearing, sight, touch, smell, taste)

Teaches creative thinking

- The hand offers opportunities to explore all of the five senses.
- **Touch:** With your eyes closed, use the fingers of one hand to touch your other hand. Feel that the back of your hand. Is it softer than the palm? Feel your fingernails. Do they feel smooth?
- **Sight:** Open your eyes and look closely at the hand you just touched. Can you see wrinkles on the knuckles? Can you see the lines on the palm of your hand?
- **Taste:** Hold your nose and lick a finger on the same hand. What do you taste? Orange juice? Jelly? Nothing?
- **Smell:** Smell the same fingers you just licked. Do you smell anything?
- **Hearing:** Finally, put the same hand close to your ear and snap your fingers or clap both hands. What does the noise you hear tell you?

Read *My Fingers Are for Touching*
by Jane Belk Moncure.

READ

Going on a Five Sense Walk

(hearing, sight, touch, smell, taste)

Teaches thinking skills

- Take a walk outside and notice the different senses you are using.
- Ask, "What do you see? What do you hear? What do you smell? What can you touch? What can you taste?"
- Start with the sense of touch. Ask your child to describe how an object, such as a rock or leaf, feels: *rough, smooth, soft,* and so on.
- Next, ask him to describe what he sees, smells, and hears.
- Last, do a taste test, although this is hard unless you are in a berry patch! You can always stick out your tongue and taste the air!

Read *Body Detectives: A Book About the Five Senses* by Rita Golden Gelman.

Count All Five

(hearing, sight, touch, smell, taste)

Teaches counting

- Make a chart with five columns.
- At the top of each column, put the name of one of the senses and a picture that represents that sense.

- Go for a sensory walk. Each time you use one of the senses, mark the appropriate column. Examples include seeing a bird, smelling grass, or hearing cars pass by.
- After the walk, count the number of times each sense was used.

Read *The Five Senses* by Keith Faulkner.

Pumpkin Fun
(sight, touch, smell, taste)

Teaches observation skills

- Ask your child what is inside a pumpkin. Cut one open and look inside at the flesh and the seeds.
- Save the pumpkin seeds. Boil 2 cups of pumpkin seeds in 1 quart of water with 2 tablespoons salt for 10 minutes. Drain and toss the seeds in 1 tablespoon of butter.
- Spread the seeds on a baking pan, and bake at 325° for 30 minutes, stirring frequently.
- Eat the delicious roasted pumpkin seeds.
- This is a great sensory experience that uses the sense of sight, taste, touch, and smell.
- **Note:** If you want to plant some seeds outside, set aside seeds for planting before you prepare them for cooking.

Read *The Pumpkin Book* by Gail Gibbons.

Our Senses for Music

(hearing, sight, touch)

Teaches appreciation for music

- Ask your child:
  - Which sense do you use to listen to music?
  - Where can you go to hear music?
  - Where can you go to see musicians play their instruments?
- Listen to a variety of music with your child.
- If possible, attend a concert with your child.

Read *Seven Blind Mice* by Ed Young.

Comparing Senses

(hearing, sight, smell)

Teaches questioning skills

- Cut out two pictures of children from a magazine.
- Compare the eyes in each picture. Talk about the shape, size, and color of each pair of eyes.
- Ask your child, "What do you think the eyes are looking at?"
- Compare the noses in each picture. Talk about the shape and size of each nose.
- Ask, "What do you think the noses are smelling?"
- Compare the ears in each picture. Talk about the shape and size of each set of ears.
- Ask, "What do you think the ears are hearing?"

Read *Mucky Moose* by Jonathan Allen.

With or Without Hands

(hearing, sight, touch, smell, taste)

Teaches awareness of senses

- Talk with your child about what hands can do. Make a list of their ideas.
- Some ideas might include picking up things, getting dressed, brushing teeth, and tearing paper.
- Talk about what you can do without your hands. Make a list of ideas.
- Some ideas might include blowing bubbles, smelling chocolate, listening with your ears, and tasting with your mouth.

Read *You Smell and Feel and See and Hear* by Mary Murphy.

READ

Name the Body Part

(hearing, sight, touch, smell, taste)

Teaches listening skills

GROUP GAME

- This is a nice game to help children remember which body part is associated with each sense.
- When you call out a sense, the children move the body part that uses that sense. For example, if you say "seeing," then the children move their eyes.
- Continue with "hearing" (move ears), "touching" (move hands), "tasting" (move tongue), and "smelling" (move nose).

Read *Busy Bunnies' Five Senses* by Teddy Slater.

READ

Five Senses Popcorn

(hearing, sight, touch, smell, taste)

Teaches observation skills

- Prepare air-popped popcorn.
- While the popcorn is popping, talk about the different senses you are using as it pops. You can smell it, hear it, and see it.
- When the popcorn is done, you can touch it and taste it.

Read *Popcorn* by Alex Moran.

Point to the Sense

(hearing, sight, touch)

Teaches listening skills

GROUP GAME

- Tell the children you are going to say a sentence that uses one of the senses and ask them to point to the part of their body that uses that sense. (For touch, they can shake their hands or feet.)
- Here are some examples:
  - Oh, look at the beautiful sky. *(children point to their eyes)*
  - This grass feels so good. *(children point to their hands or feet)*
  - Listen to the birds singing. *(children point to their ears)*
- Let one child make up sentences, and ask the rest of the children to point to the part of their body that uses the sense mentioned in the sentence.

Read *My Head-to-Toe Book* by Jean Tymms.

Make a Paper Face
(hearing, sight, smell, taste)

Teaches creativity

- ▶ Draw a face on a paper plate.
- ▶ Give your child crayons and ask her to draw ears, nose, eyes, and a tongue.
- ▶ Give her yarn to glue on for hair.
- ▶ Talk about each feature on the face and which sense goes with it.
- ▶ **Variation:** Cut out facial features from magazines and create faces using the cutouts.

Read *The Magic School Bus: Explores the Senses* by Joanna Cole and Bruce Degen.

Wheels on the Bus

(hearing, sight, touch, smell, taste)

Teaches body awareness

▶ Sing the following to the tune of "The Wheels on the Bus" and touch the appropriate part of the body as you sing each verse.

The eyes in my head can see, see, see,
See, see, see; see, see, see.
The eyes in my head can see, see, see
Every single day.

Additional Verses
The ears on my head can hear, hear, hear...
The nose on my face can smell, smell, smell...
The tongue in my mouth can taste, taste, taste...
The hands on my arms can touch, touch, touch...

Read *Arthur's Nose* by Marc Brown.

Poetry and Senses

(hearing, sight)

Teaches language skills

▶ The following is an excerpt from "Flight the Second: A Day of Sunshine" by Henry Wadsworth Longfellow.
▶ Recite the words. Then go outside and use your senses of sight and hearing to look at the trees and listen to the wind.
▶ Talk about the meaning of the words.

I hear the wind among the trees,
It plays celestial symphonies;
I see the branches downward bent,
Like keys of some great instrument,
Like keys of some great instrument.

Read *My Five Senses* by Aliki.

Green Day
(hearing, sight, touch, smell, taste)

Teaches about colors

- This fun activity can be adapted for any color. Below are examples of a "green" thing for each sense.
  - Touch—sit in the green grass and feel it on your body.
  - Sight—look for a green insect, leaf, worm, weed, or maybe a four-leaf clover.
  - Sound—hop and make frog sounds.
  - Taste—eat a pickle. Is it sweet or sour?
  - Smell—make a green salad and smell the veggies.
- Finally, ask, "If you could be green (or any color), what would you be and why?"

Read *You Can't Taste a Pickle With Your Ear* by Harriet Ziefert.

Riddles
(hearing, sight, touch, smell, taste)

Teaches thinking skills

▶ Enjoy figuring out the following sense-related riddles:
  ▸ What has eyes but cannot see? (a potato)
  ▸ What has ears but cannot hear? (a corn plant)
  ▸ What has a tongue but cannot taste? (a sneaker)
  ▸ What has hands but cannot touch? (a clock)
  ▸ What has a nose but cannot smell? (a nose cone on a rocket or the nose of an airplane)

Read *How Do We Taste and Smell?* by Carol Ballard.

Five Sense Questions
(hearing, sight, touch, smell, taste)

Teaches language skills

▶ Cut out food pictures from magazines.
▶ Look at one of the pictures—strawberries for example— and ask the following questions:
  ▸ How does it look?
  ▸ How does it sound? (What sound would it make when you bite into it?)
  ▸ How does it smell?
  ▸ How does it feel?
  ▸ How does it taste?
▶ For a perfect ending, serve the actual food for a treat!
▶ Repeat with another picture.

Read *Sensational!: Poems Inspired by the Five Senses* edited by Roger McGouch.

Comparing Senses

(hearing, sight, touch, smell, taste)

Teaches about comparisons

- Cut out pictures of animals and people from magazines.
- Compare the parts of the animals' bodies and the people's bodies that relate to the five senses.
- Are their ears alike or different? Ask the same question about the noses, the eyes, the tongue, and the hands or paws.
- This is a great way to begin a discussion of the senses.
- Glue pictures of animals and people next to one another and draw lines between the parts of the bodies that are alike.

Read *One Day I Closed My Eyes and the World Disappeared* by Elizabeth Bram.

READ

Make a Pizza Face

(sight, touch, smell, taste)

Teaches cooking skills

- Give your child half of an English muffin on a paper plate.
- Help him put tomato sauce on the muffin. Talk about the smell and consistency of the sauce.
- Help him sprinkle cheese on top of the sauce. Talk about how the cheese feels and tastes.
- Assemble many items for him to use to make a face on the pizza, such as olives, peppers, pepperoni, tomato slices, and other vegetables. As you touch the various items, talk about how they feel. They may be *smooth*, *bumpy*, *cool*, and *slick*.
- When the pizza face is completed, put the muffin into a microwave until the cheese is melted. Enjoy!
- **Note:** Always wash your hands before handling any food.

Read *Science Experiences: The Human Senses* by Jeanne Bendick.

Spring Is Coming
(hearing, sight, touch, smell)

Teaches about poetry

▶ Go outside on a lovely spring day and smell the flowers, listen to the birds, look at the grass, and feel the warm air. Talk about each sense you used.

▶ Sing or say the following poem.

Spring Is Coming adapted by Jackie Silberg
Spring is coming, spring is coming.
How do you think I know?
I smell the lovely flowers.
I know it must be so.

Spring is coming,
    spring is coming.
How do you think I
know?
I hear the birdies singing.
I know it must be so.

Spring is coming,
    spring is coming.
How do you think I know?
I see the green grass growing.
I know it must be so.

Spring is coming, spring is coming.
How do you think I know?
I feel the warm air on my face.
I'm sure it must be so!

READ

Read *Who Am I? A Book to Touch and Feel*
            by Alice Wilder.

A Mirror Game
(hearing, sight, smell, taste)

Teaches imagination

- Ask your child to look at her face in a mirror.
- Ask her to think of things she can do with her face while looking in the mirror. Ideas include:
  - Move her tongue
  - Roll her eyes
  - Puff out her cheeks
  - Wiggle her nose
  - Wiggle her ears
  - Make a big smile

Read *No Mirrors in My Nana's House* by Ysaye M. Barnwell.

Puppet Talk
(sight, smell, taste)

Teaches listening skills

- Using a puppet, give your child directions for things to do using his senses.
- Directions include: touch your eyes, touch your nose, stick out your tongue, shake your hands, and smell the flowers.
- Come up with fun things to do with one or all of the senses.

Read *The Muppets Make Puppets* by Cheryl Henson.

Questions About the Senses

(hearing, sight, taste)

Teaches sensory awareness

GROUP GAME

- Ask the children to sit in a circle.
- Tell them you are going to ask them questions. If a question applies to them, they should stand up.
- Make up questions about the senses; for example:
  - Who has brown eyes?
  - Who likes to hear fast music?
  - Who likes to taste asparagus?
- It is fun for them to see which children are similar to one another or have similar interests.

Read *One Day I Closed My Eyes and the World Disappeared* by Elizabeth Bram.

Five Senses Book

(hearing, sight, touch, smell, taste)

Teaches thinking skills

- Take five pieces of paper.
- At the top of each page, write the beginning of one sentence referring to a sense.
  - I like to see…
  - I like to hear…
  - I like to smell…
  - I like to touch…
  - I like to taste…

- Encourage your child to draw pictures that describe one sense on each page.
- Staple the pages together to make a Five Senses Book.
- Suggest that she give her book a title.

Read *Look Out for Rosy* by Bob Graham.

Pretzel Art
(taste, sight, touch)

Teaches creativity

- Put different shapes of pretzels in a bowl.
- Suggest ways your child can make designs, people, and letters with the pretzels.
- Give him a clean piece of paper on which to make a pretzel design.
- When he is finished, he can eat his design.
- Talk about how the pretzels taste. Ask, "Are they salty and crunchy?"

Read *Where Are You Going?* by Kimberlee Graves and Rozanne Lanczak Williams.

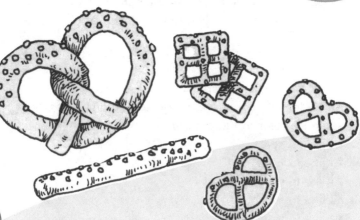

Circle Time Senses

(hearing, sight, touch, smell, taste)

Teaches body awareness

GROUP GAME

▶ Sit in a circle with the children and tell them, "We have five senses—the sense of smell, taste, sight, hearing, and touch."

▶ Say, "We see with our eyes." Ask the first child, "What do you see with your eyes?" Everyone listens to the child's answer.

▶ Say, "We taste with our tongues." Ask the next child, "What do you taste with your tongue?"

▶ Continue going around the circle with the following statements and questions:

  ▸ "We hear with our ears. What do you hear with your ears?"

  ▸ "We smell with our noses. What do you smell with your nose?"

  ▸ "We feel with our hands. What do you feel with your hands?"

Read *Toes, Ears, & Nose!* by Marion Dane Bauer.

READ

Making a Five-Sense Story

(hearing, sight, touch, smell, taste)

Teaches vocabulary skills

- Pick a theme, a time of year, or a special event, and make up a story with five sentences, each focusing on one of the senses.
- Each sentence will talk about one of the senses. For example, make your story about springtime.

When springtime comes, I see lots of green.
When springtime comes, I smell grass and flowers.
When springtime comes, I hear insects and birds.
When springtime comes, I taste strawberries.
When springtime comes, I feel warm air on my body.

Read *My Five Senses* by Aliki. READ

Variation on "Teddy Bear"

(hearing, sight, touch, smell, taste)

Teaches rhyming

▶ Say the words and pretend to do the actions that focus on the five senses.

Teddy bear, teddy bear, touch the trees.
Teddy bear, teddy bear, taste the cheese.
Teddy bear, teddy bear, smell the flowers.
Teddy bear, teddy bear, feel the showers.
Teddy bear, teddy bear, hear the singing.
Teddy bear, teddy bear, hear the ringing.
Teddy bear, teddy bear, smell the pies.
Teddy bear, teddy bear, close your eyes.

Read *You Can't Smell a Flower With Your Ear: All About Your 5 Senses* by Joanna Cole.

Identify the Sense

(hearing, sight, touch, smell, taste)

Teaches word association

- This activity offers a great way to start learning about the five senses.
- Make a chart with a picture of an eye (sense of sight), an ear (sense of hearing), a nose (sense of smell), a tongue (sense of taste), and a hand (sense of touch) on it.
- Collect pictures that relate to each part of the body and each corresponding sense.
- If appropriate, write words on index cards that relate to one part of the body or one of the senses.
- Ask a child to select a picture or word and attach it to the chart where he thinks it belongs.
- Ask him why he thinks the picture or word belongs on that place on the chart. Examples of pictures or words and where a child might put them on the chart include:
  - lightbulb, sun, flashlight—eye
  - piano, music—ear
  - skunk, flower—nose
  - apple, ice cream, hamburger—tongue
  - glove, pencil—hand
- Our senses work together let us gather information about the world.

Read *My Five Senses* by Margaret Miller or The Senses by Angela Royston.

READ

Identify the Sense

✋	
👁	
👂	
👃	
👄	

BOOKS
ABOUT THE
Five Senses

Books About the Sense of Hearing

A Day in the Life of a Musician by Linda Hayward

Annabelle's Wish: My Favorite 10-Sound Story by Michael Stewart

The Best Ears in the World by Claire Llewellyn

Bunny's Noisy Book by Margaret Wise Brown

A Button in Her Ear by Ada Bassett Litchfield

Clifford's Animal Sounds by Norman Bridwell

The Complete Book of Rhymes, Songs, Poems, Fingerplays, and Chants by Jackie Silberg and Pam Schiller

Dad and Me in the Morning by Patricia Lakin

Daisy Says "Here We Go 'Round the Mulberry Bush" by Jane Simmons

Dina the Deaf Dinosaur by Carole Addabbom

Do Your Ears Hang Low? by Caroline Jayne Church

Dog's Noisy Day by Emma Dodd

Dolphins at Daybreak by Mary Pope Osborne

The Ear Book by Al Perkins

Ears by Cynthia Fitterer Klingel

Eyes and Ears by Seymour Simon

Flop Ear by Guido Van Genechten

Freddie Frog by Emma George

Gerald McBoing Boing Sound Book by Dr. Seuss

The Handmade Alphabet by Laura Rankin

Handsigns: A Sign Language Alphabet by Kathleen Fain

Handtalk Birthday by Remy Charlip

Handtalk Zoo by George Ancona

Hear Your Heart by Paul Showers

Hearing by Maria Ruis

Horton Hears a Who! by Dr. Seuss

How to Kazoo by Barbara Stewart

The I Can't Sing Book: For Grownups Who Can't Carry a Tune in a Paper Bag But Want to Do Music With Young Children by Jackie Silberg

I Have a Sister: My Sister Is Deaf by Jeanne Whitehouse Peterson

I Thought I Heard by Alan Baker
The Indoor Noisy Book by Margaret Wise Brown
Jingle Bells by Nick Butterworth
Listen to the Rain by Bill Martin, Jr. and John Archambault
Listen! Listen!: A Story About Sounds by Barbara Shook Hazen
Listening Games for Pre-Readers by Lloyd Harnishfeger
The Listening Walk by Paul Showers
Merry-Go-Sounds at the Zoo by Patricia Benton
The Monster Book of ABC Sounds by Allan Snow
Mother, May I? by Lynn Plourde
Mr. Brown Can Moo, Can You? by Dr. Seuss
My First Book of Sign Language by Joan Holub
My First Book of Sounds by Golden Books
Night Noises by Mem Fox
Nina, Nina and the Copycat Ballerina by Jane O'Connor
Paper Cutting Stories From A to Z by Valerie Marsh
Pick Me Up! Fun Songs for Learning Signs by Sign2Me
Polar Bear, Polar Bear, What Do You Hear? by Bill Martin, Jr.
Roar Like a Lion!: A First Book About Sounds by Tiphanie Beeke
Safari Sounds: Here And There by Susan Ring
Seashells by the Seashore by Marianne Berkes
Simple Signs by Cindy Wheeler
Singing a Song: How You Sing, Speak, and Make Sounds by Steve Parker
Sound: Loud, Soft, High, and Low by Natalie M. Rosinsky
Sounds of a Summer Night by May Garelick
Sounds on the Farm by Gail Donovan
Sounds on the Go! by Gail Donovan
There Is a Carrot in My Ear and Other Noodle Tales by Alvin Schwartz
There's a Dolphin in the Grand Canal by John Bemelmans Marciano
Toes, Ears, & Nose! by Marion Dane Bauer
Too Much Noise by Ann McGovern
The Very Quiet Cricket by Eric Carle
What Do Your Hear? by Anne Miranda
Why Mosquitoes Buzz in People's Ears: A West African Tale by Verna
    Aardema
You Can't Smell a Flower With Your Ear! by Joanna Cole

Books About the Sense of Sight

"Miss Jackie's" I Love Children Songbook by Jackie Silberg
Arthur's Eyes by Marc Brown
Baby Senses Sight by Susanna Beaumont
Beverly Billingsly Borrows a Book by Alexander Stadler
Brown Bear, Brown Bear, What Do You See? by Bill Martin, Jr.
Busy Bunnies' Five Senses by Teddy Slater
Close, Closer, Closest by Shelly Rotner and Richard Olivo
Color: A First Poem Book About Color by Felicia Law
The Color Kittens by Margaret Wise Brown

Colors by Jane Conte-Morgan
The Colors of the Rainbow by Jennifer Moore-Mallinos
Estrellas Cercanas Y Lejanas/Stars Close and Far by Robin Defter
The Eye Book by Dr. Seuss
Eyes by Elizabeth Miles
Eyes, Nose, Fingers, and Toes by Judy Hindley
Goggles! by Ezra Jack Keats
Have You Seen My Cat? by Eric Carle
I Spy Little Animals by Jean Marzollo
If You Take a Paintbrush: A Book About Colors by Fulvio Testa
It Looked Like Spilt Milk by Charles G. Shaw
The Itsy Bitsy Spider by Iza Trapani
Juba This and Juba That by Dr. Darlene Hopson
Jungle Animals by Angela Royston
The Little Hands Art Book by Judy Press
Look Again! by Tana Hoban
Look Closer by Peter Ziebel
Look Once, Look Again: Animal Eyes by David M. Schwartz
Look Up, Look Down by Tana Hoban
Look! Look! Look! by Tana Hoban
Magenta Gets Glasses! by Deborah Reber
Miffy's Magnifying Glass by Dick Bruna
Mirror, Mirror by Allan Fowler
Mirrors: Finding Out About the Properties of Light by BernieZubrowski
My Mirror by Kay Davis
My Shadow by Robert Louis Stevenson
Open Your Eyes: Discover Your Sense of Sight by Vicki Cobb
Otto: The Story of a Mirror by Ali Bahrampour
Pick Me Up! Fun Songs for Learning Signs by Sign2Me
Scorpions: The Sneaky Stingers by Allison Lassieur
The Secret Code by Dana Meachen Rau
See the Sea!: A Book About Colors by Allia Zobel-Nolan
Sight by Angela Royston
Sight by Kay Woodward
Sights and Sounds: The Very Special Senses by Charles E. Kupchella
Smile-a-Saurus! A Book About Feelings by Matt Mitter
Stanley: Daddy Lion by Lara Bergen
Teeny, Tiny Mouse: A Book About Colors by Laura Leuck
The Treasure Hunt Book by Klutz
Twinkle, Twinkle, Little Star by Iza Trapani
What Does Bunny See?: A Book of Colors and Flowers by Linda Sue Park
Why the Frog Has Big Eyes by Betsy Franco
Winking, Blinking, Wiggling and Waggling by Brian Moses
You Can Use a Magnifying Glass by Wiley Blevins

Books About the Sense of Touch

Amber on the Mountain by Tony Johnston

The Barefoot Mailman by Theodore Pratt

The Chocolate Touch by Patrick Skene Catling

Clifford Counts Bubbles by Norman Bridwell

Feeling Your Way: Discover Your Sense of Touch by Vicki Cobb

Find Out by Touching by Paul Showers

Fuzzy Fuzzy Fuzzy!: A Touch, Skritch, & Tickle Book by Sandra Boynton

Fuzzy Yellow Ducklings: Fold-Out Fun With Textures, Colors, Shapes, Animals by Matthew Van Fleet

Hand Clap! "Miss Mary Mack" and 42 Other Hand Clapping Games for Kids by Sara Bernstein

Hand, Hand, Fingers, Thumb by Al Perkins

Hand-Print Animal Art by Carolyn Carreiro

Hands Are Not for Hitting by Martine Agassi

Happy Hands & Feet by Cindy Mitchell

Here Are My Hands by Bill Martin, Jr. and John Archambault

I Can Tell by Touching by Carolyn Otto

Is It Rough? Is It Smooth? Is It Shiny? by Tana Hoban

The Kissing Hand by Audrey Penn

Learning How to Use the Five Senses: See, Hear, Taste, Touch, Smell by Elizabeth Mechem Fuller

The Little Hands Big Fun Craft Book by Judy Press

Look, Listen, Taste, Touch, and Smell: Learning About Your Five Senses by Pam Hill Nettleton

Miss Mary Mack: A Hand-Clapping Rhyme by Mary Ann Hoberman

The Mudpies Activity Book: Recipes for Invention by Nancy Blakey

My Bunny Feels Soft by Charlotte Steiner

My Fingers Are for Touching by Jane Belk Moncure

My Fuzzy Safari Babies: A Book to Touch & Feel by Tad Hills

Night-Night, Baby: A Touch-and-Feel Book by Elizabeth Hathon

Oh, Baby!: A Touch-and-Feel Book by Elizabeth Hathon

Pop!: A Book About Bubbles by Kimberly Brubaker Bradley

Pure Slime: 50 Incredible Ways to Make Slime Using Household Substances by Brian Rohrig

Spiders by Gail Gibbons

The Sweet Touch by Lorna and Lecia Balian

Texture by Karen Bryant-Mole

This Little Piggy: A Hand-Puppet Board Book by Scholastic, Inc. staff

Touch by Andreu Llamas

Touch by Maria Rius

Touch by Susanna Beaumont

The Touch Book by Jane Belk Moncure

Touch and Feel Buggy Buddies: Shapes by Ant Parker

Touch and Feel: Farm by Dorling Kindersley Publishing

Touch and Feel: Fire Engine by Andy Crawford

Touch and Feel: Home by Dorling Kindersley Publishing

Touch and Feel: Shapes by Dorling Kindersley Publishing
The Very Hungry Caterpillar by Eric Carle
What Can You Feel With Your Feet? by Hertha Klugman
Whose Back Is Bumpy? by Kate Davis
Whose Feet? by Nina Hess
Wild Animals by Dorling Kindersley Publishing

Books About the Sense of Smell

Baby Senses Smell by Susanna Beaumont
Bite-Sized Science by John H. Falk
Breathtaking Noses by Hanna Machotka
Clifford Follows His Nose by Norman Bridwell
David Smells! by David Shannon
Follow Your Nose: Discover Your Sense of Smell by Vicki Cobb
Grandma, Tell Me a Story by Lynn Floyd Wright
How Do We Taste and Smell? by Carol Ballard
I Smell Christmas by Mercer Mayer
I Smell Honey by Andrea Davis Pinkney
Learning How to Use the Five Senses by Elizabeth Mechem Fuller
Little Bunny Follows His Nose by Katherine Howard
The Nose Book by Al Perkins
The Senses I Smell With My Nose by Joan Mills
Smell by Sue Hurwitz
Smell by Maria Ruis
Smell by Mandy Suhr
Smelling Things by Allan Fowler
The Stinky Easter Egg by Chris Tougas
The Story of Babar by Jean de Brunhoff
Tanka Tanka Skunk! by Steve Webb
You Can't Smell a Flower With Your Ear by Joanna Cole
What's That Smell? by Janelle Cherrington
Who's Making That Smell? by Jenny Tyler and Philip Hawthorn

Books About the Sense of Taste

Bear Wants More by Karma Wilson
Beginning to Learn About Tasting by Richard L. Allington and Kathleen Cowles
Bread and Jam for Frances by Russell and Lillian Hoban
Chocolate Chip Cookies by Karen Wagner
The Chocolate Day by Ann Herrick
Eating the Alphabet by Lois Ehlert
The Gingerbread Boy by Paul Galdone
Good Enough to Eat: A Kid's Guide to Food and Nutrition by Lizzy Rockwell
How Do We Taste and Smell? by Carol Ballard
If You Give a Mouse a Cookie by Laura Joffe Numeroff
If You Give a Pig a Pancake by Laura Joffe Numeroff

I Will Never NOT EVER Eat a Tomato by Lauren Child

Look, Listen, Taste, Touch, and Smell: Learning About Your Five Senses by Pam Hill Nettleton

The Magic School Bus: Explores the Senses by Joanna Cole and Bruce Degen

Peter's Party Senses: Taste by Sue Sherliker

Pizza Pat by Rita Golden Gelman

The Popcorn Book by Tomie dePaola

Sense of Smell by Carey Molter

Senses by Angela Royston

A Taste of Honey by Nancy Elizabeth Wallace

Tasting Things by Allan Fowler

Taste by Laurence P. Pringle

Taste by Maria Ruis

Your Tongue Can Tell: Discover Your Sense of Taste by Vicki Cobb

The Very Hungry Caterpillar by Eric Carle

Books About More Than One Sense

Arthur's Nose by Marc Brown

Body Detectives: A Book About the Five Senses by Rita Golden Gelman

Busy Bunnies' Five Senses by Teddy Slater

The Button Box by Margarette S. Reid

The Five Senses by Keith Faulkner

How Do We Taste and Smell? by Carol Ballard

Look Out for Rosy by Bob Graham

The Magic School Bus: Explores the Senses by Joanna Cole and Bruce Degen

Me and My Friend by Deborah Manley

Mucky Moose by Jonathan Allen

The Muppets Make Puppets by Cheryl Henson

My Fingers Are for Touching by Jane Belk Moncure

My Five Senses by Aliki

My Five Senses by Margaret Miller

My Five Senses by Judy Nayer

My Head-to-Toe Book by Jean Tymms

Nature Spy by Shelly Rotner and Ken Kreiseer

Night Sounds, Morning Colors by Rosemary Wells

No Mirrors in My Nana's House by Ysaye M. Barnwell

No Ordinary Dog by Mary S. Wilson

One Day I Closed My Eyes and the World Disappeared by Elizabeth Bram

Popcorn by Alex Moran

The Pumpkin Book by Gail Gibbons

The Science Book of the Senses by Neil Ardley

Science Experiences: The Human Senses by Jeanne Bendick

The Senses by Angela Royston

Sensational!: Poems Inspired by the Five Senses edited by Roger McGough

Sense Suspense by Bruce MacMillan

Seven Blind Mice by Ed Young

Thanksgiving Day at Our House by Nancy White Carlstrom

Toes, Ears, & Nose! by Marion Dane Bauer

You and Your Body: Your Senses by Dorothey Baldwin and Claire Lister

You Can't Smell a Flower With Your Ear: All About Your 5 Senses by Joanna Cole

You Can't Taste a Pickle With Your Ear by Harriet Ziefert

You Smell and Feel and See and Hear by Mary Murphy

Where Are You Going? by Kimberlee Graves and Rozanne Lanczak Williams

Who Am I? A Book to Touch and Feel by Alice Wilder

The Wonder Thing by Elizabeth Hathorn

Index

Children's Books Index

Learning Games

General Index

Learning Games